A HISTOR
REDHEATH
AND
YORK HOUSE SCHOOL

PATRICK MOORE
(HEADMASTER 1990-2005)

Published by

Triflower Press

for

York House School, Croxley Green, Herts

First Published : June 2010

ISBN 978-0-9546301-4-0

Printed by
Hobbs the Printers Ltd,
Brunel Road, Totton, Hampshire

CONTENTS

Above: Main gate in 1899 with original lions before they 'disappeared' in the 1920s

Below: The stable yard

A HISTORY OF REDHEATH AND YORK HOUSE SCHOOL

REDHEATH

Although there can be little doubt that Man has shaped this verdant corner of Hertfordshire since earliest times, little is known about Redheath's earliest history. Given its elevated situation, water supply would have been a problem hindering the first attempts at settlement.

Nonetheless, there are records of the discovery of Paleolithic flint tools at sites in both Rickmansworth and Croxley Green, while remains of a Neolithic causewayed camp, in which was found a Bronze Age axe, were also excavated in Rickmansworth. There appears to be little if any evidence of Roman occupation. Although there is no reference to Redheath in the Domesday Book of 1086, Rickmansworth was a substantial settlement by then so there must be a strong possibility that medieval peasant farmers eked an existence from their fields and perhaps there was eventually a manor here, with lord's house and demesne and peasants' strip holdings. Certainly when snow melts in the park it reveals the vestiges of ridging and ditching which characterised farming for so many centuries. We do know that by the nineteenth century the area had been turned over to wooded parkland.

Whatever manor house was here would certainly have been altered or replaced in the fifteenth century, at which time several branches of the Baldwin (Baldwyn/Baldyn) family are known to have settled in the Hertfordshire area.

REDHEATH AND THE BALDWINS

We know that the Baldwins lived at Redheath for over two hundred years although we have little concrete evidence of them. The 1525 register of baptisms at Watford parish church recorded the birth of "Henry Baldwin of Redheath". John Baldwyn lived and died there in 1570. The almshouses in Sarratt, built by him and the Baldwin family in 1550, were rebuilt in 1821.

In the chancel of Watford parish church is a stone with the inscription:

> "Here lyeth in hope of joyful resurrection the body of Henry Baldwin of Redheath in the parish of Watford, son of Henry Baldwin, a young man of espetial meeknesse and playnesse of hart, who gave his soul to God in the floure of his youth, VIZ ANNO 1601, January the last. He married Alice, daughter of Henry Martyn of Ivor and had by her three children, Henry, John and Alice. John an infant died, the others live to Gods will and pleasure. Behold a patterne of natures frayl estate when neither youth nor strengthe nor wealthe one jot or moment of time can ought prolong his date."

Thomas Baldwin died in 1639 and his monument in the Parish Church of St Peter in Berkhamsted was described in 1923 as "now in a mutilated state at the west end of the south aisle. Originally erected in about 1642 in the south transept...". In his will he left money to the poor of Berkhamsted and Watford, stating his bequests to "the parish of Watford, where I was born; to the parish of Berkhamsted where I was a scholar; to the parish of St Martin's in the Fields, where I now live". The original benefactions were derived from "springs and waters in Hyde Park" from which adjacent districts were supplied with water. These waterworks were sold in 1730 to George III since they obstructed his plans to make improvements there, including the construction of the Serpentine.

Between 1659 and 1666 Henry Baldwin bought considerable amounts of land, in the Sarratt area and that of Micklefield Hall, so that the estate was over 500 acres. In 1666 he paid tax on six hearths.

The Baldwins are still remembered locally by Baldwins Lane, running from Sarratt Road (which passes Redheath) to join the road between Rickmansworth and Watford.

REDHEATH AND THE FINCHES

In 1709 the last of the Baldwins, Thomas (son of Henry) died and left Redheath to his nephew, Charles Finch, who was the son of Charles Finch and Mary, Thomas' sister. The Finches had been a prominent Watford family for longer than the Baldwins had been at Redheath so this marriage united two important local families. In 1655 Elizabeth Finch had married John White of Bushey and her granddaughter Susannah was the mother of John Wesley, born in 1703, founder of the Methodists.

The Finch family had a pew in St Mary's Parish Church in Watford and one member of the family always served as a trustee for the Watford Free School from its foundation in 1709 until its closure in 1882.

In 1712 Charles Finch built the existing house facing west and attached to all or some of the north-facing Tudor house. Evidence of partial demolition would seem to be the use of two "double-ovulo moulded beams" (previously lime-washed) as beams to support the floor. Also, when cellars were being cleared in 1967 during the installation of mains drainage and ten years later ,when the barns were being converted, Tudor nails and hinges, as well as ancient tiles, came to light. The bolection-moulded panelling in the south ground floor room and the fielded panelling in the hall are original as is much of the upstairs panelling. The fireplace in the Entrance Hall used, as late as the turn of the century, to have "a curious old grate-back of iron. In the centre is Neptune, trident in hand, standing on a pedestal, ornamented with scallop shells. Around him are spouting dolphins and sea-monsters. Above is the date, 1724, with this inscription in Welsh...translated into 'God is our strength'" - we know nothing of what happened to it thereafter. The last of the Tudor building was demolished in the early fifties but the stables and barns, now converted to residential use, remain.

REDHEATH ESTATE : 12 OCTOBER 1760

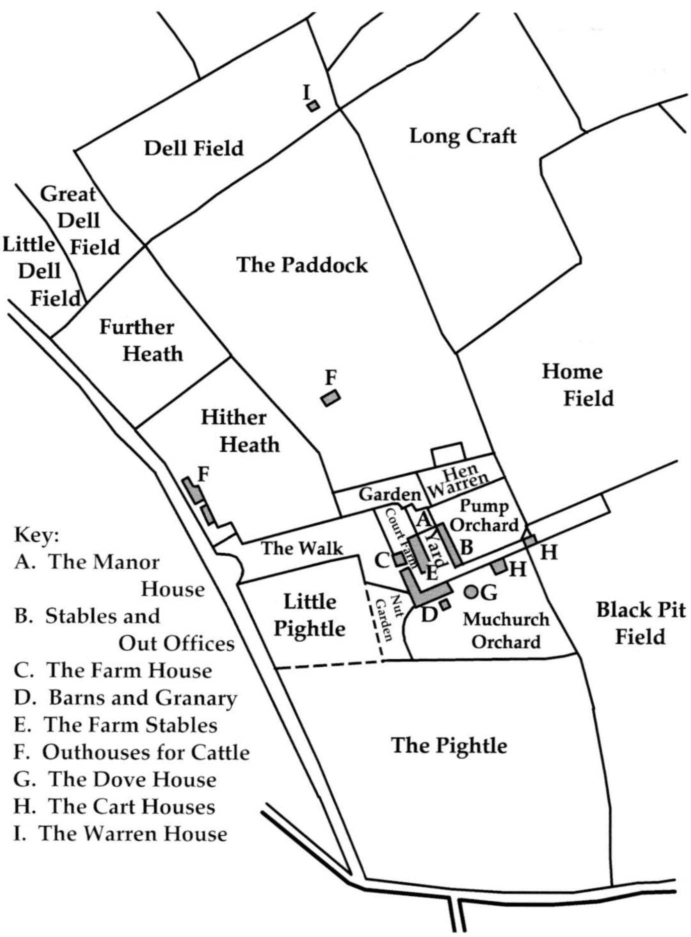

This fine building has been attributed to Sir Christopher Wren – it is perfectly possible that this was one of his last works since he died in 1723 aged over 90 (although it has been suggested that he himself did not work outside London, so it may only have been the influence of his style). Opinions conflict on this point. A Dr Campbell (Fellow in Architecture and Fine Arts – Queen's College, Cambridge) states that it is not among the currently recognised works of Wren. Mr Hall, a local architectural historian, has drawn attention to the marked similarity between the west frontage of Redheath and parts of the east side of the court of Chelsea Hospital – he says, "it is unlikely that he designed the frontage of the house at Redheath, given the late date and that Wren had virtually stopped house design work by 1711" and furthermore that the "suggestion that Wren did not work outside London is erroneous...his designs include works for the universities at Oxford and Cambridge, Greenwich Royal Observatory, Winchester Palace, houses at Kensington Palace, Tring in Hertfordshire and Winslow Hall in Cheshire". "Wren gave advice on domestic buildings and even made drawings for them although local architects, who added their own modifications, carried out the work". The design of Redheath "shows such classical simplicity that it...is more likely to have been a local architect, strongly influenced by Wren" than even Wren's son or his student (Nicholas Hawksmoor) or his assistant (William Talman).

Recently it was discovered that what looked like a barn in the adjacent property, No 2 The Stables, is in fact a late 15th century Hall House (and this building has now been accorded Grade II listing status). It "appears to have been originally built as a four-bay house with one crosswing, possibly known as Redheath Hall. In 1712 the present Grade II* Redheath was built, expressing with brick the kind of grandeur that the former hall house had done two centuries earlier". It is considered noteworthy that "instead of abandoning the timber-framed hall house" when he built a new and fashionable brick house, Mr Finch valued the original dwelling to the extent that "the four bays were dismantled and erected ...to serve as a barn". This may well not have happened for some time since there is evidence (the bleaching marks on what would have been stacked timbers) that the carefully marked timbers were removed from their original site and stockpiled elsewhere. When re-constructed the result was that, it appears, "the easternmost bay and possible crosswing to the west are no longer standing, the hall, crosswing and service end bays survive. The framing for these are relatively complete for a building originally built around five hundred years ago. The queen post with collar and single row of clasped purlins survive to each bay, some with slightly curved windbraces. The beams and posts are chamfered where they face the former hall. The longitudinal wall frames are also mostly complete with wall plate and wall posts, and to the north elevation, rails that also provide evidence of the former mullioned window (as do related diamond mortises)." "The west wall frame with tie beam has no mortises to the underside suggesting this bay communicated with the missing crosswing. The east wall frame has oweled corner posts and redundant mortises to outside indicate missing end bay. Redundant stave holes (are visible) in wall frame. Roof trusses have tie beam, 2 studs to collar supporting a single row of clasped purlins." This building was restored and converted into a residence at the start of the 21st century.

A typical 15th century hall house, reconstructed as a barn

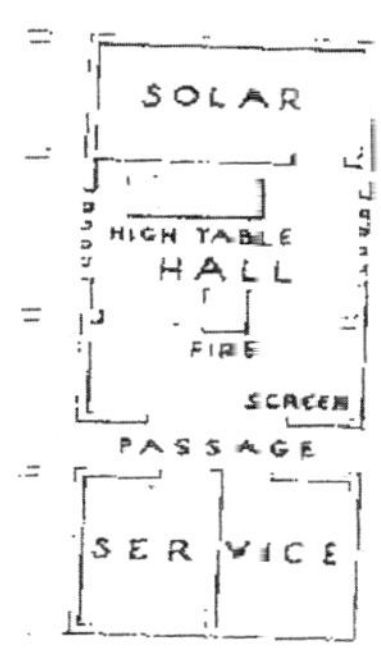

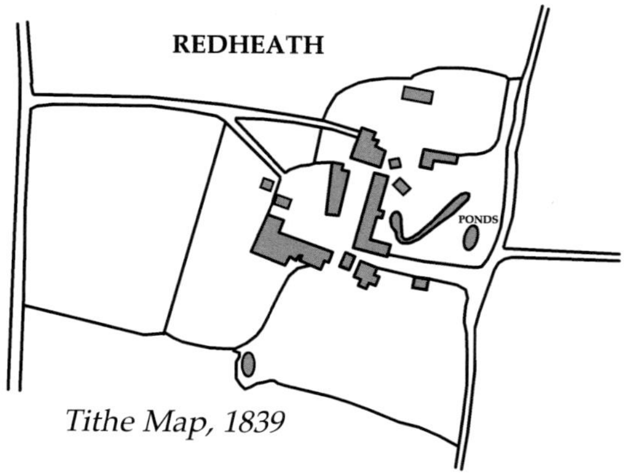

Tithe Map, 1839

In 1718 Charles Finch died without issue and was succeeded by his brother John, from whom the estate descended in direct line to Henry Baldwin Finch, whom we know was the owner in 1922, when the estate passed out of the family's possession.

In 1725 mourners were sent an extraordinary invitation, which portrayed a recumbent figure about to be buried and surrounded with lighted candles and banners and was liberally decorated with death's heads, crossed bones and a funeral procession complete with undertaker, two mutes and mourning relatives and servants. It said: "You are desired to accompany the corpse of Henry Finch, Esquire, from his late dwelling house at Redheath to the parish church at Watford on Sunday, 28th of this instant November at twelve o'clock precisely. And bring this card with you".

The cupola was added in 1743 – during alterations – and the school has on display the original clock mechanism, inscribed "Geo. Clarke, White Chapple" (see page 36). As far as the main building is concerned, it has been commented that the portico and moulded brick window cornices are of particular note as is the stone fireplace in the hall and some original 'bolection moulded fielded panelling'. It is recorded that there was, in the servants' hall, a "fine old carved table dating back to 1639" but it also is here no longer!

The bell on the stables block dates from 1853 and came from the Whitechapel Bell Foundry of John Briant, who sold it to S. Kerman & Son to place in the bell tower to replace a cracked bell. It weighed "one quarter and 25 pounds" and cost £4 3s.

In 1866 Henry Charles Finch, magistrate of Watford Petty Sessional Division, made further alterations and extensions to Redheath including a dining room and attached kitchen. Photographs taken in 1937 (before demolition of the southern elements of the building) show a double-storey building there so it seems likely that the existing single-storey building is a remnant from that demolition and the subsequent refurbishment (see later).

It is well known that the Finches planted many trees in the area around the house. Indeed in Victorian times "Finch's Avenue" was a local landmark and the source of many sketches, paintings and early photographs. At the "Clarendon Arms" one could obtain "good accommodation for your horse while you walk across a field to the left, the path through which leads to Finch's Avenue, a splendid shady promenade half a mile or so in length; under beech trees of immense height and fine growth ... the picturesqueness of which is greatly enhanced by the view in the distance of Mr Finch's mansion". It was said of it that "there are finer individual trees elsewhere but nowhere else in the county is there a beech avenue of such length and beauty". The rotted stumps of several of these trees can still be seen in the woods today.

This avenue was formerly continued towards the house by a double row of Spanish chestnuts, which were cut down at the end of the nineteenth century and replaced with fruit trees.

On the night of 13th and morning of 14th October 1881 a violent storm uprooted hundreds of trees and damaged thousands in the area. At Redheath 51 were blown down and 37 damaged, among them many in "Finch's Avenue" which was further damaged in 1918 in a severe blizzard "which seared through the Avenue leaving a trail of havoc and destruction. The ravages of nature are rapidly healed and within a few years the avenue had returned to its former glory".

In 1888 Reverend George Finch inherited Redheath and right at the end of the century it passed to Henry Baldwin Finch soon after which the Finches decided to vacate and let Redheath.

Finch's Wood, showing the avenue of trees badly damaged by storms in 1881 and again in 1918

REDHEATH AFTER THE FINCHES

We know little of the first tenants, the Peto family, clearly here only a very short time. The appearance of the name 'S.A. Peto' on the plan below indicates that it must date from their time here.

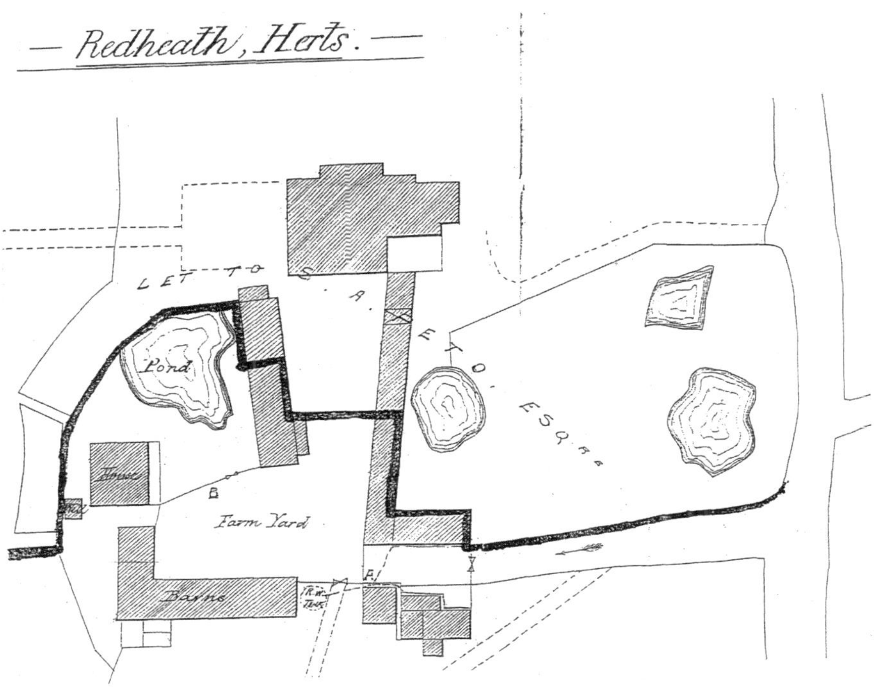

It was originally recorded that "in 1913 the house and 35 acres were leased to Mr Newall (both of whose sons were killed in the First World War) for £350 per annum, with 10 acres of agricultural land to Mr Parsons for £400 on which Mr Hickman had verbally-agreed shooting rights for £80 p.a." In addition "strips of land at Chandler's Cross, 25 feet by 40 feet, being the site of an iron church" were let to Reverend Donnell, of the Vicarage, Croxley Green, for 2/6d p.a.! We know that these tenancies ended in 1923.

However a recent visit to the site by Baroness Sharples (granddaughter of William Newall) – with a wonderful photograph album dated 1899 – has shed more light. The photographs on pages 7-15 and the paintings on 29-30 are taken from her album.

Clearly the family moved here in 1899. There were three sons: Nigel, killed serving in the Welsh Guards in 1915, Lesley, killed serving in the Royal Fusiliers London Regiment in 1917, and Keith, who served in the Royal Navy and survived to become the father of Baroness Sharples (whose brother, Lesley, was killed in World War II!). The three sculpted soldiers outside Watford Town Hall are known locally as the "Newall Brothers Monument".

Nigel's commanding officer wrote to his mother:

> Dear Mrs Newall,
>
> I cannot tell you how dreadfully sorry I am to have to tell you that Nigel was killed instantaneously on Friday morning at 5 minutes past 6.
>
> All my officers had been wounded, and he was sent to me to help me as I was in a rather bad unpleasant place with no officers. The Germans were being heavily shelled and he and I were watching from our shell hole to see if the Germans were going to retire, and we would then have shot them and followed them, and as Nigel got up to shoot at some of the enemy he was hit by a bullet in the middle of his forehead. He fell back stone dead into my arms. I cannot tell you how dreadfully sorry I am for you. He was such a splendid person and was simply worshipped by his men and loved by all of us, he will be most terribly missed.
>
> It was a great blow to both of us that he did not come to my company, but all the same we managed to see a lot of each other. I think he looked on me as his best friend, as we were the only men of the old lot left out here. It is so terribly sad I cannot get over it. We were so pleased to be together those few hours, and he behaved so well, especially as I was dead tired, and he worked very hard for me to try and give me a rest and I feel his death very deeply indeed.

(continued on page 16)

Nigel Newall

Redheath in 1899

These two pages show the estate photographed in 1899.
The house, seen from the front (above) and the north (below)

Above: The stable yard

Below: A snowy view looking down the drive from the house

INSIDE REDHEATH ...

Left and below left: Two rooms at the turn of the century whose use is not known to us

Below right: A view of the first floor landing in the late 1950s. The staircase is believed to have been rebuilt around 1950. The door straight ahead leads to the guest bedroom, now the History Room.

Above: The north lawns
Below: The kitchen garden

Stable Yard.

The stable yard, with some of its regular inhabitants

Right: The gates located at the house end of the drive

Below: The view down the drive from the house

Below right: Preparing for an outing

Left: The view of the garden from the upper floor of the house

Below: The farm

Right: The cottage in the woods – compare this with the watercolour painting on page 30

Finch's Wood after the gale in March 1918 *(see page 4)*

The post is just going, so I must hurry up with what I have to tell you. He was buried yesterday morning a hundred yards from where he fell. After he was killed I went through his pockets to send you back anything. As I was doing so a shell burst and knocked me and my orderly over and buried us, so I fear that some of the few personal private effects that he had with him are lost. I know there was a small pig that he loved, but it was buried, also his watch. The orderly was taken straight to hospital, I shall go to see him to-day and find if he saved anything. The only things I have were his identity disc and his cigarette case, which if you will allow me to, I am very anxious to keep till the end of the war, and if I get killed I will see it is returned to you. I fear this letter is very disjointed, but I've only just come out of the line. We have had the hardest time I have ever had and for once I feel rather shaken and most terribly sad.

With my love and my very deepest sympathies.

Yours very sincerely,
Percy Baltye

PS I particularly want a photograph of Nigel if you would be kind enough to send me one. I will write again tomorrow. Just before he was killed, we were talking about home and other things, and his last words to me about one minute before he was killed were: "Thank God, Percy, we are out here, and not winning the war in England."

Map of the estate c.1923

THE EBURY YEARS AND AFTER

In 1921 the third Lord Ebury died and his brother was forced by death duties to sell the family home, Moor Park Mansion. He bought Redheath in 1922 for £27,000 including 475 acres (from Rousebarn Lane and Redhall Lane across Sarratt Road to Little Green Lane and Bell Wood). He attached an aviary to the kitchen garden. Some confusion surrounds what happened to the gates at this time. It is known that the rampant lions (or were they griffins? – the Finch coat of arms was "argent a chevron between three griffins passant sable") on the columns of the gates were replaced by the Ebury dogs and a wrought iron working of the Grosvenor family sheaf of corn placed above the entrance (see page 23) so it seems that the actual gates were also replaced since the Finch family's gates showed "a black boy being swallowed by a snake".

In 1932 Lord Ebury died. Redheath passed in trust to Rt. Hon. Robert Egerton, Baron Ebury and was let to Mr Hutchinson until 1937 when the fifth Lord Ebury came of age and "promptly sold the estate to Mr C.H.Burne of Lincoln's Inn for £49,000" – this figure must have included all 475 acres, since the house and 60 acres were later sold for £16,000. Development into a high class residential estate was planned but this was abandoned when the area was zoned part of the Green Belt.

The caretaker in 1937 was Charles Cole, who had just retired after forty years as a City of London policeman. His granddaughter recalls happy times spent at Redheath: "We played in the summer house and nearby we paddled in the fish pond and spent carefree days exploring the extensive grounds. My grandfather shot rabbits and pheasants on the estate and my grandmother prepared and baked them. She was an excellent cook so there was always the aroma of bread and cakes from the Aga. There was a high wall surrounding the kitchen garden from where we picked peaches. Oh, such halcyon days!". Inside the house was perhaps not so pleasant: "There was no electricity so oil lamps were used and candles in holders for the long trek to bed, casting eerie shadows! A large barn full of coal was found and used in all the living rooms and bedrooms in use".

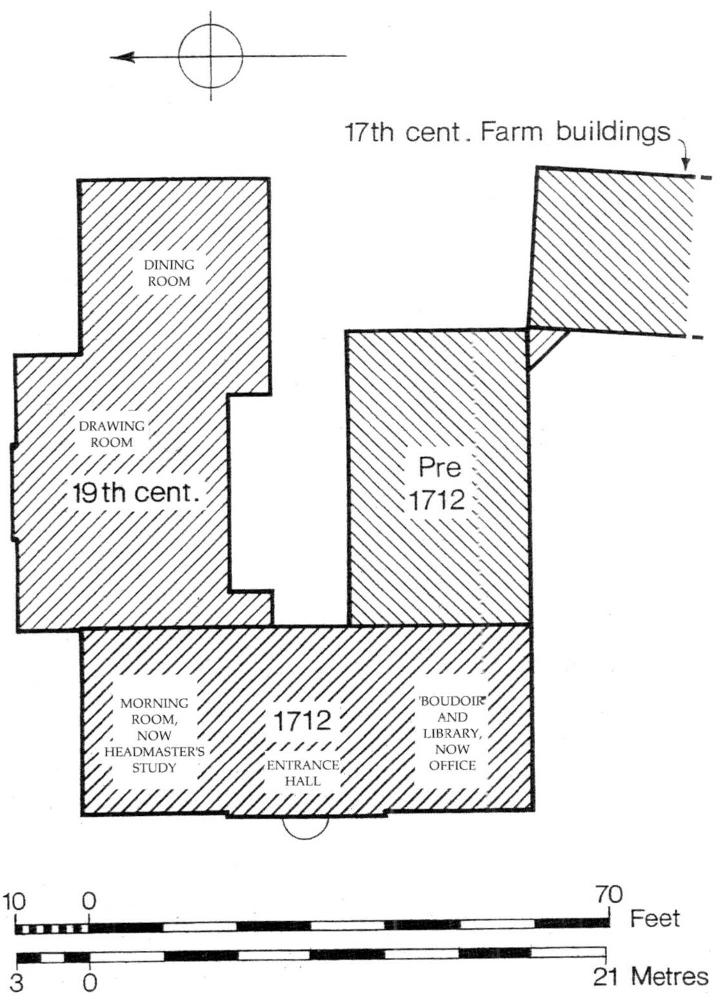

This and following page: Floor plans produced in connection with the 1937 sale, that on this page showing the position of the 19th century wing demolished in the 1950s.

SECOND FLOOR

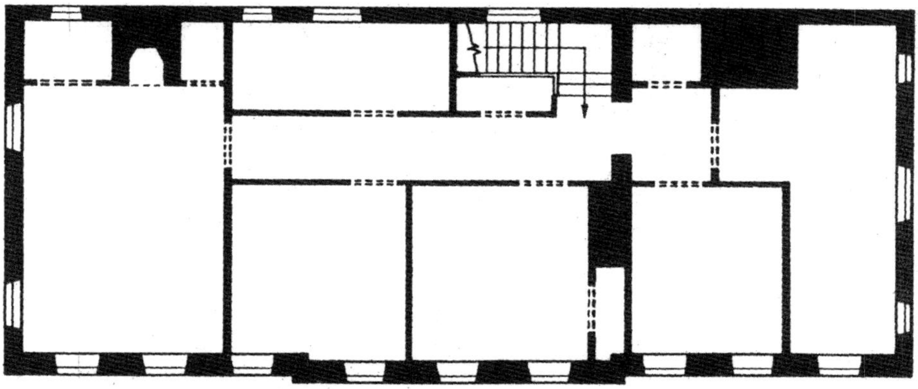

FIRST FLOOR

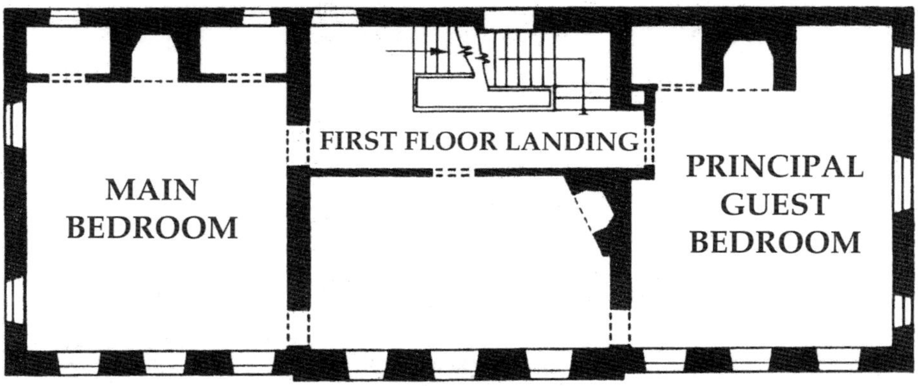

GROUND FLOOR

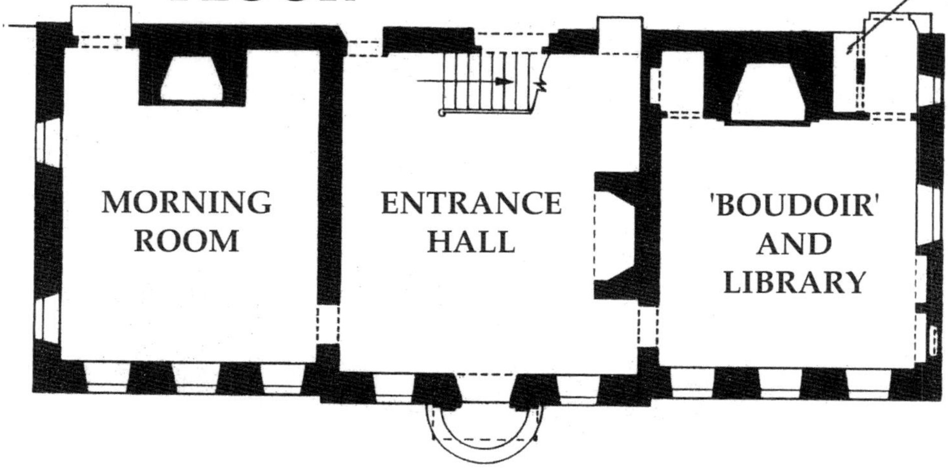

By direction of The Lord Ebury.

Redheath

CROXLEY GREEN, HERTFORDSHIRE

Stations : Croxley Green 1½ miles.
Watford 2½ miles.
Rickmansworth 1¾ miles.

An Exceptionally Fine Queen Anne Residence
the original part said to have been built
by Wren in 1712

Sole Agents :
Messrs. ALFRED SAVILL & SONS, 51a, Lincoln's Inn Fields, W.C.2. Telephone : Holborn 8741.
Messrs. JOHN D. WOOD & CO., 23, Berkeley Square, W.1. Telephone : Mayfair 6341.

Pp.19-22: The four-page sales brochure produced for the 1937 sale

REDHEATH

is of most attractive appearance and is built of mellowed red brick with a tiled roof, having a Clock Tower centred over the Porch.

A gravelled Drive 200 yards in length leads to the Residence which contains the following accommodation:

Entrance Hall

with large open stone fireplace and panelled walls. Off this open the RECEPTION ROOMS as follows :

Morning Room

19ft. by 17ft., with open fireplace.

Boudoir

17ft. by 16ft. 9in., panelled in chestnut. Inset on one wall is a range of sunken bookshelves. Open fireplace, door to Cloak Room and Wine Cellar, cupboard by fireplace.

Drawing Room

which is also approached from the Lounge Corridor. This room is about 31ft. by 20ft., having mellowed panelled walls and ceiling in the Adam style, open fireplace, and French windows opening to terrace.

Dining Room

about 26ft. by 19ft. 3in., having open fireplace and serving hatch.

A Passageway leads to :

Gun Room

adjoining this is Cloak Room and Lavatory, and

Smoke Room

26ft. 8in. by 19ft. 2in., with open fireplace, range of bookshelves, and French windows.

The Reception Rooms are light, lofty and very well proportioned.

The Offices

are well shut off and include : Servants' Hall, a large light Kitchen, Scullery, Pantry, Larder, built-in plate safe, Butler's Pantry, etc., good Cellarage, Servants' Staircase.

The Principal Staircase rises from the Lounge Hall to the *FIRST FLOOR.* Off the Corridor open :

Eight Principal Bed and Dressing Rooms

A Bath-Dressing Room and a Second Bath Room

and W.C. Housemaid's Pantry. One of these rooms has probably the original pine panelling of the period.

ON THE SECOND FLOOR:

Day and Night Nurseries

WORK ROOM. NURSERY BATH ROOM. TWO MAIDS' BED ROOMS.

Shut off, and approached by the Secondary Staircase, are :

Four Servants' Bed Rooms and Servants' Bath Room

Water Softening Plant in the roof.

Company's Water is connected. Electric Light from Private Plant. Drainage to Cesspool. Central Heating is installed.

Conveniently adjoining, are Garage for three cars with covered washdown. Engine House for electric light plant. Game Larder with Man's Bed Room over. Bothy containing Four Men's Rooms. Stabling comprising Four-stall Stable, Six Loose Boxes, Forage Store, Harness Room, and Three-stall Stable.

Gardens and Grounds

The Grounds surround the house and include, in addition to the Parkland, wide expanses of Lawn, a newly constructed Sunken Garden, Rose and other Flower Gardens, Ornamental Trees and Shrubs, Hard Tennis Court, a fine walled Fruit and Vegetable Garden, a large Cherry Orchard.

In the Gardens are a double spanned heated Greenhouse and a Lean-to House, Forcing Frames, etc. A brick and tiled Range of Garden Buildings.

The Home Farm Buildings

which are situated near the Residence, include BAILIFF'S HOUSE. Cow standing for 6 (in range of Stabling), a timber and felt Garage, a timber and tiled open Cart Shed with lean-to Dairy and Cooling House, Two Barns, a four-bay open Cattle Shed, Granary, a two-bay open Implement Shed, standing for four cows, and ditto for eight, a newly constructed range of Nine Piggeries, and an underground Fruit Store; and North of the house are a Four-bay Open Cart Shed, a Trap House, an open ditto, a Two-stall Stable and Two Loose Boxes, Two Loose Cattle Boxes with enclosed yard, and the Estate Stores.

In addition there is a well-built LODGE, at the entrance to the Drive.

FOR SALE FREEHOLD WITH ABOUT 60 ACRES.

Price, £16,000

Fixtures and Fittings at valuation.

FURTHER LAND MIGHT BE PURCHASED.

Photographs on this page and pages 24-26 taken in 1937:

Above: The house as seen from the main gate on Sarratt Road

Below: Boudoir and Library (now School Office)

Above: Morning Room

Below: Drawing Room

Above: Entrance Hall

Below: Principal guest room, now the History Room

Above: The stable yard

Below: The garden and kitchen garden

Article in the Watford Observer reporting the dry rot threat to Redheath, with a photograph showing the extent of damage to the roof and fabric of the building.

"Redheath," Croxley Green, one of the county's showplaces, is in the hands of housebreakers. It is a victim of dry rot.

4126

END OF A STATELY ENGLISH MANSION

ANOTHER of the Stately Homes of England will soon be nothing but a memory. "Redheath," Croxley Green, is in the hands of the house-breakers, being demolished because of the ravages of dry rot.

In August, 1948, Watford Rural Council, who had requisitioned it, hoping to use it to relieve the housing shortage, decided to free it, but expressed anxiety that it should be preserved because of its architectural value, and sought the guidance of the Ministries of Town and Country Planning.

Experts have been over the mansion, but could advise nothing except that it be levelled.

SHOW-PLACE OF THE COUNTY

The mansion was built in 1713 for Mr. A. Finch, and stood in 700 acres of beautiful parkland and woodlands. It was one of the show-places of the county. Fringing the roadway to Sarratt was a cherry orchard, now in a state of decay, but once a delightful sight in the spring.

Another feature of the grounds was an avenue of trees more than half a mile in length known as Finch's Avenue. This was ravaged in a blizzard in 1926.

GHOST OF A PET SHEEP

The old house had its ghost story—the apparition of a pet sheep which was said to have haunted one of the landings.

Mr. G. E. Neale, the caretaker, who until recently lived in part of the mansion, when questioned about the ghost, told a "Post" reporter:

"My wife and I did not hear anything, but our son tells us he used to hear strange noises and was often conscious of a presence which he could not explain. He never saw anything as far as we know. . ."

In a matter of weeks, the old house, scene of so much old-world splendour, will be levelled with the dust. The bricks and woodwork will be carted away and "Redheath" will be no more—just a memory of the days when the squire held sway.

Where it stood, maybe a new housing site will take shape, and, who knows, children of another generation will play at lords and ladies—unaware that their childish fancy will have a foundation of fact.

During building works in 2001 a large rectangular pit (27ft x 11ft) was discovered in the old kitchen garden. It was lined with "semi-engineering bricks (waterproof)" with a concrete floor laid on brick rubble and a reinforced concrete roof entered by an unusually large manhole cover. It was clean and not smelly so cannot have been a soakaway. At the time various theories were put forward. It was felt to be too well constructed to be a holding water cistern for the kitchen garden or to be a cold store. It was thought possible that it might be an English Resistance bunker – we were told that Anthony Quayle, the actor, was a Major in the Royal Artillery and that he and his team had the job of going round the country setting up these bunkers (containing stores of ammunition etc.) in case of German invasion. More recent discovery of the 1937 sale brochure seems to indicate it may have been a store for fruit and vegetables. It is now under the new Pre-Prep and Kindergarten building, so we shall probably never know!

In 1938 Watford District Rural Council were hoping to buy the whole estate for preservation but this proved impossible as the Second World war loomed and the park, farmlands and woodlands which made up the estate were sold off. The Peninsular and Oriental Steam Navigation Company planned to buy Redheath and some of its land – for £16,000 – as part of its contingency plans should war break out, but it is not clear whether they ultimately bought or leased it in 1939. Accommodation for men and women on the staff and telephone connections having been arranged, part of its London offices was evacuated here as a precaution against bombing – their records were stored in the capacious cellars and in horseboxes (removed from their ships) around the grounds. Redheath also became the headquarters of the local Home Guard.

P&O stayed at Redheath until 1946 after which the house was left deserted and increasingly derelict and overgrown. Lead thieves stripped part of the roof, dry rot set in particularly at ground level and it seemed that nothing could save the house from an ignominious end. Watford Rural District Council again made several attempts to save Redheath – by trying to get "various ministry Departments interested in this building with a view to its preservation" – but to no avail and was eventually, with great reluctance, obliged to grant a demolition order.

At the eleventh hour a Sarratt builder, Mr Downer, who was also Chairman of the Watford Rural District Council, persuaded Mr Geoffrey Allen to buy Redheath which he did, with the help of Mrs Martha Childs, "a London lady particularly interested in the preservation of historic buildings" and the Georgian Group, in November 1950. The sad state of the place is reflected in the price – £2,500 for the house, "partly demolished", and nine acres.

Described as "one of the finest gems of Sir Christopher Wren's architectural genius" in the Watford Observer article about the saving of Redheath, the building was only saved after the last minute intervention of Mr T.C. Downer. "Anxiously aware that demolition was immediately threatening Wren's historic treasure", he approached Mr Allen "one Sunday in January to urge that something must be done at once, feeling that Mr Allen, as a lover of this type of building, would endeavour to save at least Redheath's fine façade". Upon realising that demolition had begun next day, Mr Allen "called on the P&O Line to start negotiating for purchase on condition that demolition be halted immediately but the following evening Mr Downer telephoned Mr Allen in London to say that demolition was still proceeding, part of the roof of the Wren building having already been stripped off". Mr Allen rushed back from London to his farm in Sarratt, "mustered his farm workers and with them reached Redheath early next morning before the demolition men could get their hands on another brick". The "narrow margin" by which Redheath was saved from being "levelled with the dust" is shown by the fact that "the clock and chimneys had been sold and were due to go that day. The panelling of the rooms had been disposed of to the Savoy Hotel, who, after Miss D'Oyly Carte's help had been enlisted and promptly given, readily cancelled the deal".

It is interesting to note that another Watford Observer article mentions that "somewhere about 1866 a wing, three times as large as the original house, was added" and also that "dry rot had seriously attacked the Victorian wing".

It had always been understood (before this article came to our attention very recently) that the "Wren building" was a west-facing extension to a previous north-facing Tudor/Elizabethan building (which had been added to the original Hall House) – and that it was customary in the early 18th century that, if the owners could not afford to rebuild completely, a "Georgian exterior cladding" might have been applied to the rest. The 1949 photographs on pages 33-34 would seem to support "the 1866 theory" and it may be that we simply do not yet have the relevant records of a demolition of the timber framed building and rebuilding in the form of the "Victorian wing". Part of the confusion may arise from the fact that it has always been known that bricks and timber from Redheath were used in a 1950s extension of neighbouring Oak Farm (by Mr J Downer), after demolition of part of Redheath at that time. However there can be no doubt as to the Tudor and Elizabethan dating of the stable block and old barn.

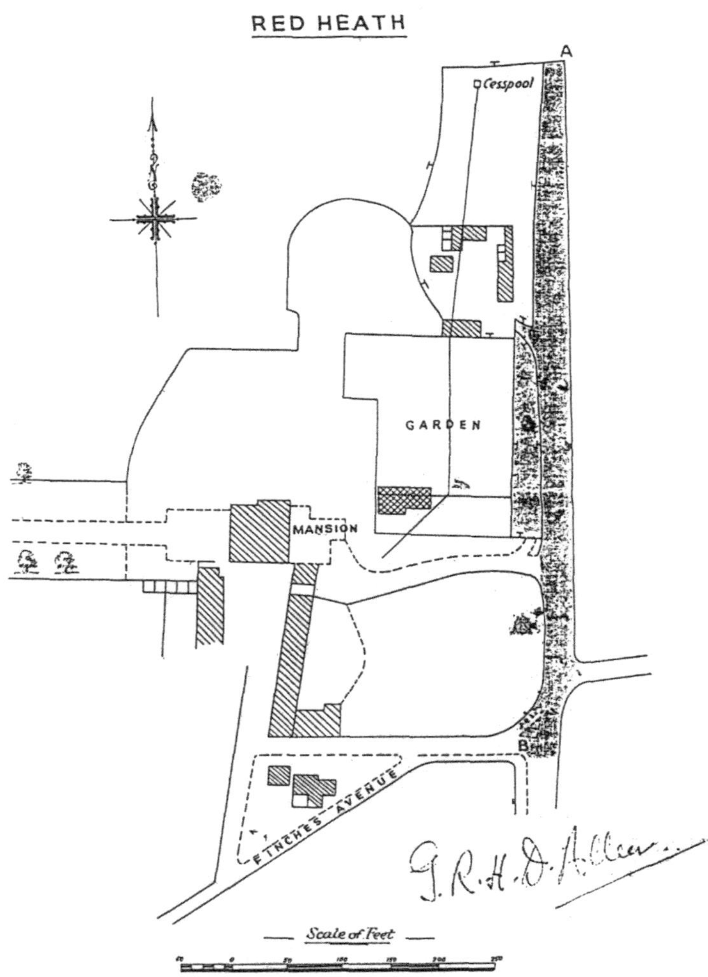

A plan presumably dating from around 1949, bearing the signature of 'G.R.H.D. Allen'

Contemporary watercolours which also appear in the photograph albums:

Above: Entrance to stable yard

Above: The cottage in the woods (see also photograph on p.14) Below: The garden with sundial

Above: Aerial view of the school and its neighbours in 1995

Below. Aerial view in 2008,
showing the extent of the three major new buildings erected between 1997 and 2005

In 2001 the old Pre-Prep building (above) was replaced by the new Kindergarten and Pre-Prep building (below)

This page and overleaf: Four photographs taken in 1949
Above: The front
Below: The rear, taken from the stable yard

Above: Looking into the stable yard from the west

Below: The north wing (partly demolished soon afterwards)

Mr Allen clearly never intended to live at Redheath and sold off most of the land as well as "Tythe Barn" (most of the Tudor and Elizabethan barn) and "Bailiffs House" and "Redheath Lodge". He then sold Redheath to Mr Somerset who continued the restoration work and also managed to buy back 58 acres of the original park although he sold just over two acres to Mr Downer in May 1952 to add to Oak Farm behind the school.

Mr Somerset was unable to complete the restoration programme he had planned and in 1952 sold the estate to Lord Poole, former Chairman of the Conservative Party and Head of the Central Office, for £13,750. He bought back the area of land which now comprises much of the main school playing field. The following year a large part of the estate was leased to Mr Saunders of Model Farm for £65 p.a.

Lord and Lady Poole were responsible for further internal work and all the remaining Tudor and Elizabethan parts of the old house at the back were demolished (and, it is said, material incorporated in Oak Farm nearby) to the extent that where there had been 30 bedrooms there were now only seven! The gardens had gone wild and had to be restored on a smaller scale (in 1935 there had been seven gardeners but Lord Poole had only one, Mr Alan Thornton whose wife, Bella, was a long-serving and excellent cook for the Pooles). Lord Poole had a sunken garden built near the tennis court, the design having been shown at Chelsea in the fifties. (When York House moved here it was hoped to turn it into a swimming pool but the brickwork was too severely frost-damaged so it was filled in).

Harold Macmillan visited while Prime Minister – along with masses of extra telephone lines to link him with Washington and Moscow – and "Thornton", who ended his days as York House caretaker, liked to recall serving early morning tea in bed to Edward Heath in what is now the History Room!

The History Room opened onto the landing of the main staircase. There is an old legend, in connection with the old staircase, which echoes "some old tragic history". The exact story we have not been able to confirm but a lady who used to visit has confided to us that she always felt the shivers when she climbed those stairs"!

In 1966 the history of Redheath, "standing with poise and dignity at the end of a shady drive of spreading elms", moves into another phase as part of the history of York House School.

Lord Poole's Dining Room, in the north wing of the building

Above: The original 1743 cupola clock mechanism inscribed "Geo. Clarke, White Chapple"

Below:
The original cellar. The exit sign dates from the wartime Home Guard use of the building and marks the old coal chute

YORK HOUSE SCHOOL 1910–1966

The earliest school group photograph, dating from 1911

York House School was founded in September 1910 by Rev. Cambridge Victor Hawkins (known respectfully and affectionately as 'the Owl' – because of his wisdom and not his appearance!) at 98 Broadhurst Gardens, Hampstead. He either came from, or had lived in, Wimbledon and that proximity to the Wimbledon Tennis Club is apparently the reason for the school colours. The school crest – the crossed keys of St Peter – may reflect time spent in York or simply his calling (although it is almost certain that he only took the cloth at least ten years after founding the school). To him we can also reasonably assume that we should attribute the school motto – "aut viam inveniam aut faciam", meaning "either I shall find a way or I shall make one". Interestingly, the same Latin inscription is to be found on a portrait of Robert Sydney, brother of Elizabeth I's favourite, Sir Philip Sydney, in Montacute House in Somerset.

The school was housed in what was "an ordinary semi-detached suburban house with a back garden converted into a hard playground. Behind the rear garden fence ran the Great Central railway track from Marylebone Station and beyond that the Metropolitan Railway. The trains were a constant delight to many of us" with a better view of the locomotives when they were coming south and slowing down before entering the station.

The playground was something like a terracotta tennis court but the surface was not so smooth. Both before lessons and during morning break – when a glass of milk and three Petit Beurre biscuits were rapidly consumed – football or cricket took place, both games played with an old tennis ball. Injuries were treated "with red carbolic soap – and in my mind I can still almost feel the resultant stinging".

SPEECH DAY,

DECEMBER 19, 1914.

YORK HOUSE SCHOOL,

HAMPSTEAD

"Aut viam inveniam, aut faciam."

HONOURS LIST.

St. Paul's School -	Foundation Scholarship -	W. D. H. Beyts
University College School -	Exhibition -	C. A. Sansom
Highgate School -	House Exhibition -	H. F. R. Sturge

PRIZE LIST.

Form Prizes.

Upper IV. - - - - - - - - H. H. Michael
(Presented by ARCHDEACON HUNT.)

Lower IV. - - - - - - H. H. A. Warneken
(Presented by Mrs. EDWARD MICHAEL.)

Upper III. - - - - - - - N. A. P. Godhard
(Presented by ALFRED HAYSMAN, Esq.)

Lower III. - - - - - - - J. N. Cohen
(Presented by Mrs. MICHAEL MOSES.)

Forms II. and I. - - - - - J. Druiff and T. Ito
(Presented by The HEAD MASTER.)

Best Average without otherwise obtaining a Prize
J. A. H. Shankland and R. N. Cohen
(Presented by Mrs. JOHN LANCASTER.)

Special Prizes.

Scripture - - - C. A. Sansom and H. S. P. Moses
(Presented by Col. W. G. Beyts, R.A.M.C.)

Classics (Seniors) - - - - - - C. F. L. Holford
(Presented by CHARLIE STURGE.)

Classics Juniors - - - - - - H. F. R. Sturge
(Presented by STANLEY HOLFORD, Esq.)

Mathematics (Seniors) - - - - - H. H. Michael
(Presented by H. K. PICARD, Esq.)

Modern Languages - - - - - - A. E. Cohen
(Presented by N. D. GULLICK, Esq.)

French (Juniors) - - - I. M. H. Wilson and A. Harris
(Presented by the HEAD MASTER.)

Drawing (Seniors) - - - - - - C. A. Sansom
(Presented by the HEAD MASTER.)

Drawing and Writing - - - - J. M. Jeffery
(Presented by The HEAD MASTER.)

Writing (Seniors) - - - - - - C. F. L. Holford
(Presented by The HEAD MASTER.)

General Knowledge - - - - - - D. P. Woolf
(Presented by the HEAD MASTER.)

Music - - - - - - - R. R. Seitz
(Presented by Miss HAWKINS.)

Head Master's Prize for Boarders - - - E. Warneken

PROGRAMME

PART I.

DISTRIBUTION OF PRIZES

BY THE

VENERABLE ARCHDEACON HUNT.

INTERVAL.

PART II.

PIANO SOLO - - Tarentella - - *Jean Doustē*
R. R. SEITZ.

DUET - - - Barcarolle - - - *Hoffmann*
The Misses LEWTHWAITE.

SONG - "The Nightingale of Lincoln's Inn" *Herbert Oliver*
Miss LILLIAN POLKINGHORNE.

SCENE from Molière's "*Médicin malgré lui*"

Sganarelle -	M. M. Shimberg
Valère - - - -	H. H. Michael
Lucas - - - -	C. A. Sansom

ARGUMENT.—Valère and Lucas are in search of a famous doctor, and meeting Sganarelle's wife (who has just received a beating from her husband) are told by her that Sganarelle is in fact the doctor in disguise, and that he must be thrashed until he confesses his identity.

SONG - - The Blind Ploughman *Coningsby Clarke*
Miss DAISY LEWTHWAITE.

SONG - Waltz-Song from *Romeo and Juliet* - *Gounod*
Miss LILY LEWTHWAITE.

SONG - "Come out, come out, my dears" - *Dessauer*
Miss LILLIAN POLKINGHORNE.

SCENE from *The Acharnians* - - - - *Aristophanes*

Dicaeopolis - - -	C. F. L. Holford
Euripides - - - -	H. F. R. Sturge
Servant - - -	H. H. A. Warneken

ARGUMENT.—Dicaeopolis applies to Euripides, the creator of many woe-begone characters, for the loan of some property-rags that his appearance may excite pity in the hearts of the judges at his coming trial.

DUET - - - "I heard a voice" - - *Glover*
The Misses LEWTHWAITE.

SCHOOL SONG AND CHORUS The King's Song - - *Sullivan*

At the Piano - - Miss HAWKINS.

GOD SAVE THE KING.

The programme for the school's Speech Day, 1914

Midday dinners were "happy occasions" with "'The Owl' presiding and carving large joints of beef accompanied by the best Yorkshire pudding I have ever tasted".

The earliest school group photograph we have – dated 1911 – shows 31 boys and four staff and one taken only a few years later shows 41 boys, six male staff and five female (some of whom look so young as to have been pupils, but were in fact a matron and classroom helpers)! Seated in the middle is Mr J.H. Turner, joint Headmaster until about 1912.

Swimming (in the summer) and gymnastics (in the winter) lessons took place at the Hampstead Baths in Finchley Road. Sergeant Macpherson taught swimming – "he walked along the edge of the bath holding a long pole with a large loop at the end of it, into which I inserted myself, and, supported by the loop around my midriff, probably made far too frantic breaststrokes. Now and again, and hoping I would not notice, he would lower the pole and consequently the loop – and with it my support – resulting in momentary panic". Cricket and football took place on playing fields belonging to University College School – to get there necessitated a long walk, in "crocodile", including a path through Hampstead Cemetery!

In about 1928 the school moved to 1 Crediton Hill in Hampstead. The Senior Master was Mr Baron, known to staff and boys as "M'Lord Bushey" (where he lived).

Soon another move occurred, to 1, Lymington Road.

A newspaper cutting of 30th July 1931 recalls a cricket match between the School and Old Yorkists on the University College playing fields at which a presentation was made "amidst prolonged applause" to 'the Owl' to celebrate 21 years as Headmaster and "as a mark of the high esteem in which they held him". The nature of the gift is not recorded but "if the size of the gift were to be taken as the measure of esteem, no room would be large enough to hold it" so it was "thus only a token" – it may have been a "radio receiving set".

We know of some of the staff at the time. Mr George Rust, who taught English, "had a famously short temper and I am afraid we tried hard to make him explode", "had a penchant for green ink, always finishing a script with the sign of a green fish" and was the Scout leader, who took boys to "camps at Alfriston and Clovelly and a trip to Lundy Island on a paddle steamer"; a Mr White was a Latin scholar and "with Rev. Hawkins tried to imbue us with classical learning"; Mr Viscount taught French and History; Sergeant Keegan taught boxing and fencing. Another popular member of staff "a caricature of a Prep. School master" was Mr Hazeman: "unkempt hair, large round spectacles, a long grey moustache, a gown that had seen better days. He couldn't keep order but was a good teacher – when he had the opportunity! He was apt to put his pipe in his jacket pocket when it was still alight!". Mr Davison "taught Maths and used to drive an ancient motorbike which looked at least as old as he was!".

YORK HOUSE SCHOOL.

Drill and Gymnastics.

APRIL 3rd, 1935

Seniors, Formation Drill - - -	Sergt.-Major Kirk.
Juniors, P.T. and Marching - -	Sergt. Adderley.
Seniors, P.T. and Marching - -	Sergt.-Major Kirk.
Juniors, Gymnastics - - -	Sergt Adderley.
Seniors, Figure Marching - -	Sergt.-Major Kirk.
„ Pommel Horse - -	Sergt. Abbot
„ Box Horse - - -	Sergt Penning.
„ Agility - - - -	Sergt.-Major Kirk.
High Jump - - - - -	Sergt Abbot
Tug-of-War - - - - -	Sergt Penning.

PRESENTATION of CUPS and MEDALS.

Jacobs Cup for Leader - - -	A. R. Herbert.
Senior Challenge Cup - -	G. W. Dayer-Smith.
Nancy Michaelson Cup - -	P. H. Herbert.
Junior Cup - -	B. J. Woolf.
Trevor Gush Cup for Boxing - -	D. C. Richfield.
Runner up, Seniors - -	D. E. Stone.
Runners up, Juniors -	J. M. Gillingham-Diss. H. I. Goldman.
Special Medals. - - - - -	K. L. Manning. J. G. Arnold. P. E. G. Lawrence. C. A. Maclean.
Improvement Medal - - -	J. B. Cohen.
Junior Squad Medals. - - -	A. Frais. A. H. Isaac. C. Berline.
Fencing Medal. - - - - -	R. N. L. Simmons
Games Badges.	P. H. Herbert, B. J. Woolf, J. O. Buzzacott, J. Joseph.

MEDALS AND CUPS PRESENTED BY THE REV. THE HEAD MASTER, MR. & MRS. KEEGAN, MISS M. BOWMAN, MR. & MRS. M. JACOBS AND BY THE OLD YORKISTS' CLUB.

Below: The roll of honour for Sports Day, 1935

Left: 26, Maresfield Gardens, Hampstead with (below) the Headmaster's Note in the October 1937 issue of The Owl *reporting the school's change of address.*

By 1937 the school was at 26, Maresfield Gardens, in Hampstead NW3. The Rev. Hawkins is remembered as "a High Churchman", who burnt incense at his services but whose "main claim to fame was that his sermons lasted only five minutes. As a result his church was always full and not only of Christians". He is recalled as "round-faced and bespectacled" (although another Old Yorkist never saw him wear spectacles) and it is also noted that "two women taught the younger boys and administered discipline with the aid of an old gym slipper"!

The accounts for the year ending 5th April 1937 make interesting reading. Fees' income was £2030. Wages were £177 & salaries £786! Lighting and heat cost £36 and repairs only £20! Total expenditure was £1507 13s, giving a profit of £522 7s.

The Head Master's Notes

Avete:—S. A. Sandelson, A. Coller (Summer, 1937) J. B. Elkan, M. Horowitz and M. Kaye.

September, 1937, is for York House a date comparable to 1066 or 1485 in English History, for it witnesses a new period in the life of the School. Not only does a new school year begin now, but it begins in a new house, and with a newcomer writing these notes. Yet just as the history of the English People continues whatever the historians may say about certain sharp dividing lines, so does York House go on this term; its traditions are still handed on, and its aspirations for the future remain the same.

The School's new home is at 26, Maresfield Gardens, N.W.3, and I hope and believe that this will be found a place convenient to reach and healthy and pleasant in which to work (and play!)

With regard to the retirement of the Founder of the School, I have known him for so short a time, and Old Yorkists have known him for so long, that it would be presumption on my part to write about his work here. I should, however, like to add to the tribute that will be found elsewhere in this number, that I have received every possible kindness and assistance from him at this time of change-over, and I hope that " The Owl "—if I may now call him that—will still look upon York House as a place which always keeps " open house " for him.

615

Rev. Cambridge Victor Hawkins, Headmaster, 1910-1937

At this time Rev. Hawkins either became unwell or tired of the venture and sold York House – the school but not the building – to Mr Arnold George Francis White, recently acting Headmaster at Malsis Prep. School in Yorkshire, where he had taught before teaching at Charterhouse. Prior to going to Oxford between 1919 and 1921 as a Classical Exhibitioner, he had served in Flanders as a Royal Field Artillery officer.

A letter from Truman and Knightley, "Scholastic Agents", dated 27th August 1937, says Mr White should "pay one and a half terms' fees for the goodwill of any boys transferred to you; a rental of £200 a year with a full repairing lease, 7, 14, or 21 years; and the sum agreed of £50 for the School furniture". We are fortunate to have the draft letter of Mr White's final offer and Rev Hawkins' acceptance (dated 21st August, 1937, and at a lower price than Mr White suggested) – "my man and wife have now told me they will not remain next term. I cannot face the servant problem again at my time of life. I am willing, therefore, to accept...I am confident that a youngish man with plenty of enthusiasm will do very well indeed here."

Mr White described the school as "one of a row of houses, pleasant but quite unsuitable for a school – several floors and a basement, and a long narrow garden: 'the Owl' had sold his previous house in west Hampstead before finding a replacement and in desperation had to take what he could find"! Mr White had had to insist in his final offer that Rev Hawkins "redecorate those rooms that need it before I take over or to allow me to redecorate them myself and to deduct an agreed sum, say £30, from the first half year's rent in respect of the cost of this".

Mr White translated the School motto as "Research and Resource". There were 42 boys and two masters – "one good and one hopeless at keeping order" – and "a very efficient secretary, horrified at the change of heads". She was Mrs McMillen but was known for the very many years she had been secretary as Miss Florrie Dickery (her trophy for the "Inter-House Athletics Challenge" is still in use). A Maths master, Pre-Prep. mistress (for two boys?) and Woodwork teacher were quickly recruited for the Autumn term.

From about 1920 the school magazine, called *The Owl*, was edited by the Old Yorkists, the last issue, number 58, being produced in May 1939. Only two copies have come to hand – the 1949 editor states sadly that all his copies were destroyed in the Blitz.

Issue No. 54 (February 1938) mentions a total of 48 boys and contains an advertisement for "School Outfitter: Joseph Moody, Hosier and Hatter, 171A Finchley Road – four doors from the Hampstead Swimming Baths". Issue No. 57 mentions that Singing and Natural History were introduced as regular subjects on the timetable but there were now only 38 boys, some boys having already been evacuated due to the threat of war. The Old Yorkists' Club had presented 'the Owl' with a wireless to take to his new country parish of Hannington, where he had also been appointed Chief Air Raid Warden.

As war clouds gathered on September 28th 1938, following "a fierce speech from Hitler", Mr White wrote to his wife of his concerns about the possible need to arrange evacuation: "parents began to be alarmed at the prospect of staying in London (the Jews especially)...Miss Dickory was at her wits' end to know how to keep the parents quiet...if war came not more than half a dozen parents proposed to let their sons come to YHS. ... but a large majority hoped the school would move to a safe spot bodily, so to speak, and carry on as a boarding school". It was planned to move to Wiltshire and "at the parents' request to bear part of the cost incurred in making the contingency plans to evacuate, 7s 6d was added to each school bill".

A "house at Great Missenden was too expensive...it was also empty and I saw no hope of improvising school furniture for a long stay". He even considered amalgamation with his old school, Malsis. However salvation was at hand: "an Old Boy came to drive us anywhere we wanted to go – most extraordinarily decent of him – so Miss Dickory and I went off into Hertfordshire to find some places...most had already been snapped up – some by schools – and they were not overclean either!".

Mr White – although "personally I hate being uprooted and don't think London too unsafe – but other schools are going" – decided to join the London County Council evacuation programme, having abandoned the idea of moving to Wiltshire since "private transport would be almost hopeless to arrange".

THE OWL

Vol. 9—No. 53 October 1937

Editorial

The Editor and all readers of this Magazine will wish to express their affectionate farewells to The Owl on his retirement from the Headmastership of York House School.

For over twenty-five years the Rev. C. V. Hawkins has been known by a wide circle of people as " The Owl." This circle included many besides the boys and their parents, and it speaks volumes for the respect in which The Owl is held by all who know him, for it has become forgotten as a nickname and is used rather as a term of respectful and affectionate greeting. We hope that the title of the Magazine may remain as a mark of that affection.

The new Headmaster, Mr. A. G. F. White, comes to us with a glowing recommendation from The Owl, and we welcome him accordingly. " Good luck, sir, and may the School continue to flourish in the new house and under its new Headmaster and truly live up to the York House motto:—
" Aut viam inveniam aut faciam."

The Owl *reports the retirement of Rev. Hawkins, the school's founder and Headmaster for the first twenty-seven years.*

Left: The cover of the February 1938 issue of The Owl.

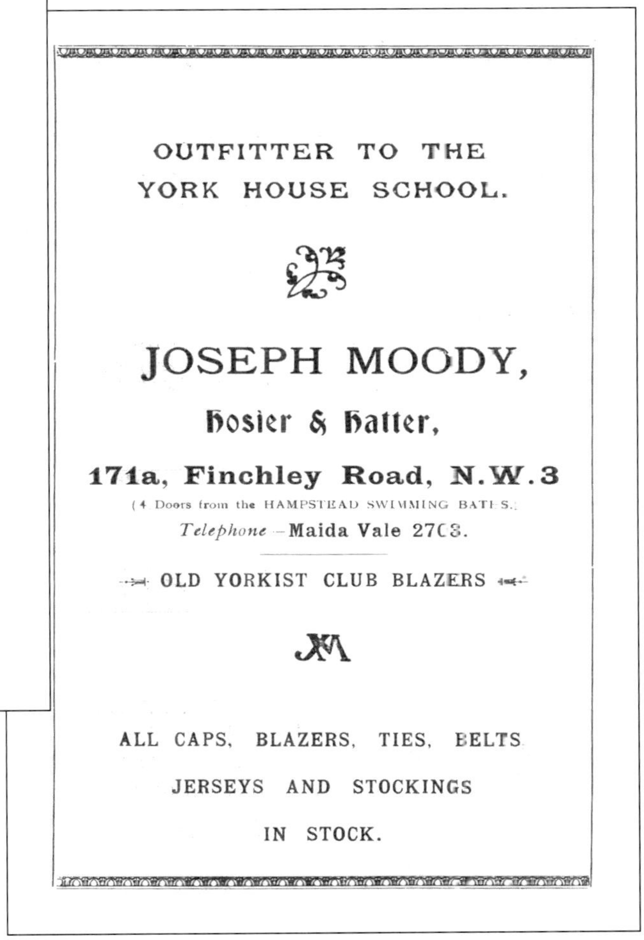

Right: Advertisement for Joseph Moody, the school outfitters, which featured regularly in the pages of The Owl *during the 1930s.*

Every morning for a week in September 1939 the school assembled and eventually all were marched to the station and taken by train – "into very distant and safe country. Cornwall perhaps or the Midlands? No, to Rickmansworth, just 17 miles from dangerous London!". At first welcomed and billeted in scattered houses this was not a problem since it was still officially holiday time – Mr White and the boys met in a local hall and went for walks. Just after term had officially begun and makeshift lessons were under way. Mr White was able to rent "Cremore" at 10, Cedars Avenue from where it is thought he soon spread into no. 12 – certainly the large double garden became "a pleasant playground". Only 22 boys remained, all that had survived the upheaval of the move.

At this time – when Mr White was on night duty three nights a week as an Air Raid Warden – his diary records that on 5th January 1941, "nearest so far, a bomb fell near Batchworth Lake, 300-400 yards from the school" and a bomb, "thrown overboard by a bomber fleeing London", fell on a house at the far end of the road, occupied by two pupils and their parents, luckily with no injuries.

Three other diary entries reveal his attempts at normality despite all: "30th January – football for the boys (there were 30) with enemy planes overhead hidden by low clouds and bombs falling on Watford; 10th March – bombs on several days this week; 18th March – beat Beacon School, Amersham 3-2"!

Above: School group c. 1920 (see page 39)

Below: School group 1938, at the start of Mr White's headship

The school's preparations for war are reported in The Owl, *February 1939*

> The last crisis (it may be the " last crisis but one " by the time you read this) found us ready to turn ourselves into a boarding-school in the country if war came. Unless I was much mistaken, I noticed considerable regret among a good many boys when they realised that their country " holiday " was not coming off ! I should like to offer my grateful thanks to all those—and they were many—who helped, or gave promises of help if it should be needed, at that difficult time.
>
> Our Christmas Dinner pursued the usual course of such affairs on Thursday, December 15th, when thirty-two—the largest number since I first came here—sat down to table. We were very pleased to see " Miss Goodwin " with us again. After we had gone, as it were, from Pudding Lane to Pie Corner, school caps gave way to more seasonable wear, but the more sober headgear came into its own again during the walk to the Heath and back which took the place of first lesson in the afternoon.

In early 1942 a Miss Hennings decided to sell up and move further away from the bombs so Mr White acquired her Meadow Way School and all its boys (and a few girls), paying £150 for the goodwill. The summer term began with juniors at Meadow Way (50 boys and 14 girls) and seniors (30 boys) in Cedars Avenue. Thus this amalgamation raised numbers "from 54 to 94 at a stroke". A pupil recalls Mr White as "tall and stooping with curly grey hair. He was of course a figure of some awe to a 4–7 year old. Unfortunately my only actual memory is scoring 1 out of 10 in a Geography test conducted by Mr White!". More diary entries tell us, "29th May – caned three boys for fooling in the street: 8th June – John Surrey won £40 p.a. scholarship to Merchant Taylors' (the school's first) – whole day holiday to celebrate".

Meanwhile Mr White's diary records that in March 1942 Rev. Hawkins had sold 26 Maresfield Gardens for £2350 – "it is almost incredible" (to sell a London property for that price in wartime). It seems that Mr White had paid rent on the house meanwhile. In the first Rickmansworth prospectus fees were:

"Boys over 8 years of age: 15 guineas per term
Boys under 8 years of age: 12 guineas per term
The following are optional:

Dinner (5 days a week): £4 10s per term	Boxing (10 lessons): 1 guinea per term
Dinner (4 days a week): £3 12s per term	Carpentry (12 "): £1 10s 6d per term
Occasional dinners: 1 s 9d	Swimming (10 "): 1 guinea per term"

The Meadow Way building (left) acquired by the school in early 1942, together with 40 former pupils of Meadow Way School. This building was used by the junior school, with senior pupils housed in the Cedars Avenue building.

The Autumn term began with 97 pupils (still 14 girls) but was soon rocked by the news that Mrs Phillips, the owner of "Cremore", the Cedars Avenue building, gave three months notice to the school to quit since she needed it. "Alternative properties were immediately investigated and Meadow Way was put on the market with the intent to find one building big enough to amalgamate the school". An extension was granted for the Spring Term and then, as a result of "14th April 1943 – Phillips v White, Watford County Court – due to be heard at 1215 but in fact heard all afternoon 2.00–5.30 – verdict for the plaintiff with costs but YHS given four months to find somewhere to move to". Provisional notice was given to the parents that the school would close in July if alternative accommodation could not be found. A frantic search for new premises began: "14th May – went round Moneyhill ... hostile reception – many lies about the premises. Beetles, mice, rats, ghosts!!; 21st May – 100 parents attended a meeting at Meadow Way and gave a vote of confidence to AW to do what he thought best" – the resolution, passed unanimously, stated: "that in view of the services Mr White has rendered to the parents, we assure him of our confidence and support in all plans he may make for the future of the school". Eventually the Ministry of Works in Cambridge, where Mr White had travelled "to tackle them in person but was refused an interview – 'all appeals in writing!' ", granted licence for repairs necessary on Money Hill House early in August, enabling the school to vacate the other two premises, storing furniture in Money Hill House's lock-up garages.

Money Hill House was about a mile from the centre of town, standing back a little from the road from Uxbridge to Denham. This building was said "to have been originally a Dower House and Cardinal Wolsey himself had slept in it" – although mainly Georgian, built in 1722, with a fine façade, it had "an attractive Elizabethan hall and fireplace and a good Jacobean staircase".

Several eminent townspeople had previously lived there: William Plaistowe, "a partner in the Rickmansworth Bank which failed in 1826"; then Thomas Fellows, "its attorney, brought up a family ... trained in law and high class cricket"; Hon. Reginald Capel, son of the Earl of Essex and Director of the Great Northern Railway; Thomas Andrews, designer of the "Titanic" who went down with it in 1912. Coincidentally Lord Ebury is also thought to have owned it late in the 19th century.

Money Hill House

Left: The entrance hall

Opposite:
Above: The front
Below: The rear

Behind it "were really beautiful grounds – a large sunken lawn, big enough for school functions (including, soon enough, dramatic productions), with a wisteria covered wall on one side of it, and on the low bank which surrounded the lawn a splendid and very ancient tree – a pseudo-acacia I am told, almost as old as the house" – and there was also "a front garden and wide lawns for games." The house had two floors and the two very large rooms became a classroom/dining hall and a Hall/music room. The enormous cellars served as air raid shelters.

The building had previously been a nursing home and then "it had for some time been run, very unsuccessfully, as a hotel by two elderly ladies, who were in continuous trouble over their lack of black-out precautions", and who kept, it was said, 23 cats. Once too a goat is said to have been met descending the stairs. It can very easily be imagined that an immense amount of work had to be done to get the whole place ready for a school. Despite this the school was only a couple of weeks late opening for the Autumn Term 1943! Mr White's diary tells us, "30th August – in possession of MH at last. Roof in bad state; 30th September – WE MOVE! All day job, no gas; 6th October – repairs more or less finished. Autumn term started with 97 pupils – same as last term; 13th November – parents allowed to visit the school 2-4pm: very successful".

By Easter 1944 there were 104 pupils most of whom were vaccinated due to a smallpox scare. On 15th June we are told "about 11.30pm, red glare, enormous explosion which I saw, the house rocked. Next morning found French windows open and one big window in Assembly room broken. Glider bomb at Mill End". Despite the very frequent air raid alerts (and "at least 40 killed by a bomb in Watford" on 29th July) all Common Entrance candidates were successful and one scholarship gained, a new bicycle rack for the boys delivered, several inter-school matches were played and "successful senior and junior plays and Christmas Carols in Mill End Church Hall". Michael Shoesmith and Malcolm Bates were awarded scholarships to Merchant Taylors'. Fees were now between £5 10s 6d and 10 guineas.

Numbers rose steadily and Autumn Term 1945 saw 123 boys. The decision to remain in Rickmansworth after the war and not to return to Hampstead was clearly the right one, the school was duly "recognised as efficient by the Board of Education" and began to compete increasingly successfully for local scholarships. In April 1946 "Mrs Shuster owner of Money Hill House offered it for sale to AW for £7000" but there is no further mention of this until 1951. In November 1946 there was a "Senior Parents' meeting – first in the history of the school. Well attended (50-60). Very interesting discussion. Many good (and some futile) points raised. Discussed wealth, homework, swimming, scripture, respect of small boys for older ones, buses, bicycles, behaviour, changing".

1947 was clearly a difficult time for reasons Mr White graphically explains, "27th January – boys milk froze all week, lavatories and basins froze, there were cuts in electricity and gas and coke for the boilers was in very short supply". In February "33 degrees of frost was recorded one day" and frequent burst pipes while in March there were "official inter-house snowball fights"!

The school magazine, now named *The Yorkist*, reappeared in December 1949. It records the death of Rev Hawkins in June of that year, having last visited the school, "though obviously ill...because he wanted to be with the school again and was afraid that he would not see another year go by", sometime late in 1947. The same issue records Nigel Ransome Williams being placed at the top of the Merchant Taylors' list with a major scholarship worth £60! There were now 135 boys. Mr Cant, who was to become Senior Master and move with the school to Redheath, joined the staff.

In May 1951 was "the first wet Sports Day since 1938" and in November the purchase of Money Hill House was completed but not before consideration of the purchase of Scotsbridge House which "had the River Chess running through it...expensive and probably unsuitable".

In September 1952 there were now 147 boys and Mr White recorded that he "brought the school register up to date – there have now been 534 boys at the school since I took over". *The Yorkist* of 1952/3 indicates that although the Physical Training Display was still one of the year's highlights, boxing no longer formed part of it (although boxing did continue as an 'extra' until 1964). It also contains a graphic account – by twelve year old N. Quin – of the Stars and Stripes system at the time. At House meetings if you had six stripes or more, the Housemaster uttered "the fatal words": "Six stripes, eh? You have qualified for the hot seat". You were then sent to the Headmaster where you joined the queue of boys and awaited your turn

THE YORKIST.

Vol. 1. DECEMBER, 1949. No. 1.

THE REV. C. V. HAWKINS

HEAD MASTER 1910-1937.

DIED JUNE 6TH, 1949.

It is indeed regrettable that among the events of the past year the first "Yorkist" has to record the death of the founder of the School, the Rev. C. V. Hawkins. We had been delighted to see him at Prizegiving in 1947, when, though obviously ill, he had made the long journey from Shanklin because he so wanted to be with the School again, and was afraid that he would not see another year go by. His fears were only too well founded, and at Prizegiving this year the Head Master paid the following tribute to him :—

There is, however, this year one very sad event, not actually in the School but intimately connected with it, which we have to record, and that is the death of the Rev. Cambridge Victor Hawkins, far better known as the 'Owl'. So well known indeed was this nickname that people have often asked me, "Now, tell me, what *is* the 'Owl's' real name?" I well remember the first time I met him; I looked round his study, and there were owls everywhere—book-rests, paper-weights, and so on—and, as he saw me looking at them, he smiled and said, 'They call *me* 'The Old Owl'. I'm supposed to be wise, you know.' And so he was wise. He founded this school in 1910, in West Hampstead, and carried it on with great success until he retired in 1937."

The Head Master then went on to speak of the 'Owl's' later work as a clergyman, and as an honorary chaplain to the Forces, and concluded :—

"Even after the 'Owl' had retired, he continued to take the deepest interest in what was going on here. In fact, I think that in secret, right up to the end, he always regarded York House as 'my school', and I am glad that he did so. My wife and I feel that we have lost a very dear personal friend, and I know that everyone connected with York House will share this feeling. The thing that struck me most forcibly, when I met those who had been at York House in the 'Owl's' time, was the great affection with which they regarded him, and it was clear that this affection was felt not only by the boys but by their parents. It seems to me that a man who can inspire such a feeling in those among whom he lives and works, even though he moves only in the small circle of a school such as this, has not lived his life in vain."

The Yorkist*, successor to* The Owl*, reports the death of Rev. Hawkins in 1949*

as you listened to "the swishing of the cane and the cries of agony" of those ahead of you. (This 'automatic' system ended in 1963!). The cricket team had "a bad season scoring 11 against St John's, 15 against Wellington (away), 26 (Russell 21) against Terry's and against Wellington at home all out for 7, our worst!".

In 1953/4 *The Yorkist* editorial says that "television, although useful as a rather transient aid to knowledge, is certainly no substitute for reading"! That of 1954/5 celebrates forty years on the staff as secretary and bursar, of Miss Florrie Dickery (Mrs McMillen). 1954 on the School Honours Board has the name J.E. Sulston (a major scholarship to Merchant Taylors') – he was knighted in 2001 for his work on the human genome project and subsequently awarded the Nobel Prize for Medicine in 2002. Mr White's diary for 1955 includes "14th June - cricket v Terry's tie 33 each; 23 June – beat Wellington by 8 wickets, first school win for three years!" and "18th November – OY Dinner at Bedford Arms, Chenies. 11 present...roast duck, sweet, chocs., coffee: 10s".

In November 1956 the school was inspected by HM Inspectors and was "recognised as efficient". The report records 158 boys (an increase from 136 since the last report in 1950). Fees were now 17 guineas a term for senior boys. Buildings, rooms and equipment were generally satisfactory and there was "a 16mm sound projector, and a portable gramophone, but no radio or filmstrip projector"! There were "three masters and five mistresses...a stable and competent staff...there is a sense of purpose behind the work that is done which communicates itself to the boys". There were seven prefects. The conclusion read, "This is a school which has a strong spirit of self respect and in which relationships between staff and boys appear to be good. The school is faithfully serving its specific purpose of preparing boys for other schools and is also cultivating some of the interests that are of value to the development of its pupils". In the same term the school "had the most formidable and successful XI in its history, all school matches being won... by at least three goals" – the following two seasons they were also unbeaten!

Games took place on the fields near Scotsbridge Mill. Meanwhile swimming continued to be very popular at Watford Baths where the school had started to go in 1949.

One long-serving member of staff was Mrs Marjorie Wraith, "who would be best remembered as Form Mistress of IIB...and also taught Botany throughout the school". One of her opinions on teaching was "Boys never give much trouble; it is the parents who cause the real problems".

As the school moved into the Sixties the editorial of the 1959/60 *Yorkist* stated that "no boy leaves this school whose moral and spiritual fibre is not strengthened by the influence of Mr White". At Speech Day, celebrating the school's golden jubilee, the guest of honour was an Old Yorkist and senior London magistrate, Mr HFR Sturge, who told the boys, "What we must try to do is find what we are good at, measure ourselves and go to it". At the end of 1960 Mr White converted the school into a Charitable Trust "in order to secure the future of the school" with the Headmaster of Merchant Taylors', Mr Hugh Elder, very soon following Mr McMillen as Chairman, since also in 1960 "Miss Dickery's service to the school, begun in 1915" was terminated by her sudden death. Also appointed to the Board at this time was Mr Bernard Ratcliffe, who served the school superbly until 1993. At this time there were 148 boys, rising to over 160 by the time Mr White retired in 1963. Shakespearean plays were very much the order of the day, the first two being "Macbeth" and "Hamlet".

In 1962 the first May Fair was held – to begin to raise money for a Jubilee Hall – and it raised £556. At Speech Day in 1962 Mr White announced that in future two periods of Science per week were to be taught in response to its introduction into the curricula of preparatory schools. He cautioned that "what must be guarded against, in this scientific snowball, is the feeling that Science, either as research or technology, has all the answers. Enormous good has come from extending the bounds of knowledge but if great values be now discarded, Science, so far from giving us pleasure will bring us nearer the dust bowl" – recall that he was a Classics scholar!

After 26 years Mr White decided the time had come to retire in 1963 so he sold the school, "price with goodwill, £15,000". In a letter from the Chairman of Governors, Mr Elder, he was told, "You have given the best years of your life to York House and its boys and its reputation is your reward". He maintained his connection, as President of the Trust, "until age and distance from Norfolk made regular attendance difficult". Mr Arthur Joseph Archdale, succeeded him as Headmaster.

An unknown and undated play in the garden of Money Hill House

Arnold George Francis White, Headmaster, 1937-1963

Educated at Marlborough College, Mr Archdale saw service with the Royal Artillery during the second World war, rising to the rank of Captain. He served in North Africa and then, following the Anzio Landings, took part in the advance through Italy, including the battle at Monte Cassino. After the war he studied mathematics at Aberdeen University, where he met his wife, Sheena, whom he married in 1950. He then taught at two prep. schools before his appointment to York House in 1963. A passionate life-long follower of cricket, who had captained his university team, he had been advised at a young age to forfeit his promising golf career as that would affect his cricketing skills. He was also passionately fond of teaching and "his classroom timetable was always full. He and his wife were regarded by staff and parents as a formidable team and were devoted to the welfare of the school and its pupils. It was also believed that the couple's high teaching standard (she taught French) greatly contributed to the school's academic standards".

Almost at once Mr Archdale was faced with serious problems with the fabric of the school building, not least of all the roof! This required urgent renewal at the impossible cost of £10,000. Furthermore in his first term the Public Health Inspector visited and condemned the school kitchen. An agreement, which ended up lasting for 17 years, was entered into with Hertfordshire County Council whereby meals were purchased and ferried from the William Penn School kitchens (unless they were on holiday when "cuisine Archdale was on offer"! – interestingly the expenditure for two days in 1964, for 120 boys plus staff, was £10 17s 2d!).

Consequently the Governors began to seek an alternative site, planning to sell Money Hill House rather than attempt the repairs. Since rumours were rife about the future of York House time was of the essence. Several possibilities were investigated and because of the urgency much was made of the merit of Great Sarratt Hall – it "certainly was a beautiful little country property but not ideal for conversion into a prep. school" – but the situation was resolved when the school was gazumped in September 1964! At this time Mr David Davies, Latin teacher and later Senior Master, joined the staff.

Finally Money Hill House – "the clustered building - about the Tudor Hall with its Queen Anne façade and the gracious gardens beyond" – was sold for £70,500 and Redheath, with 48 acres, was purchased for £45,000 (the owner, Lord Poole, wishing to make a quick sale).

YORK HOUSE MOVES TO REDHEATH 1966

Much work had to be completed on the house itself not least of all structural work in the cellars and on the ground floor (thanks to dry rot) and the removal of the original, and very beautiful, staircase (thanks to fire regulations and dry rot!) and the building of its replacement to the rear of the house. Attached to the gracious building were the Arnold White Hall (opened by Mr White himself at Speech Day in 1966), classrooms, dining hall and "well-equipped changing room, complete with showers. No longer will York House boys have to return home carrying with them the mud from the games fields!". Existing rooms were adapted as additional classrooms and Headmaster's accommodation, study, office etc. Mr Ratcliffe, an architect and governor, put in an enormous amount of hard work to facilitate the move and to establish the new facilities – he was appointed Chairman in 1967.

Much work was also needed on the grounds. While much was done by outside contractors, "Thornton", who had stayed on at Redheath after the death of his wife and the departure of Lord and Lady Poole, assisted a succession of groundsmen and gardeners – he remained a loyal servant of the school, latterly as caretaker, until his death in 1989, after 38 years at Redheath. Mr (gardening, cleaning and boilers) and Mrs (cleaning and dinners) Roberts were other loyal servants of the school – they started at York House in 1958 and she moved with it to Redheath, retiring in 1972. Although in the Sixties Hertfordshire primary schools had been greatly improved and "were, indeed, considered to be amongst the best in the country" a change to "modern methods" occurred at the end of that decade, encouraging parents to flock to the 'independents', as a result of which York House's numbers rose from 150 to 250.

Work starting on the Arnold White Hall 1966

Retired Headmaster Arnold White at the 1966 Speech Day (right) presenting a pupil with a cup.

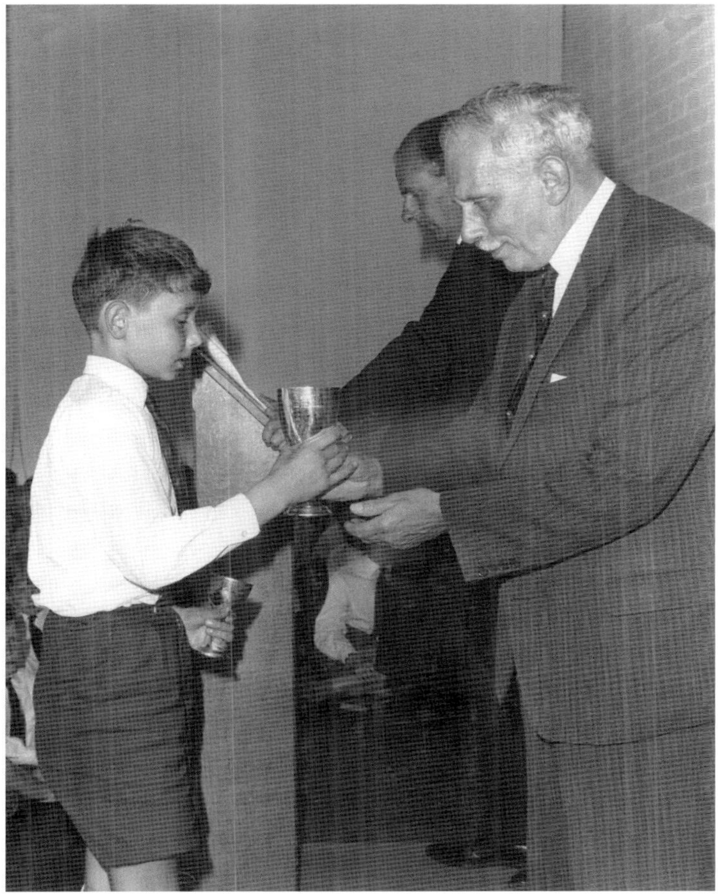

The main reason for his presence was to open the newly-constructed hall named in his honour (left).

This in turn led to further development and expansion of the facilities which was later taken still further in the "heady days" of the prosperous late Eighties.

1968 saw the opening of the new Pre-Prep. Department. The assembly of the pre-packed units in the enormous, old and fertile kitchen garden was a source of great interest to their future occupants – it was surely a most welcome change from being housed in the dining hall! Fees were now £50 per term.

1971 saw the opening of a new classroom block, which included science, art and handwork rooms, following an appeal organised by the parents. 1974 saw the completion of the staff block and also the retirement of Mr Cant, earlier Senior Master, and Mrs Wiles, a junior form teacher, both after 25 years' service to the school – "both were typical post-war teachers who came in as amateurs and became professional through experience. Generations of boys remember their classes with pleasure". Fees were £90 per term.

In 1977 the school became much warmer when the old night-storage heaters were replaced with an oil (now gas) fired central heating system Fees had risen to £185 per term. In 1978 "the Magnificent Seven", the entire scholarship form, gained awards not least of all due to the expert teaching of Mr Archdale himself – this was followed, the following year, by Mr Archdale's announcement that "never before has the school done so well in the academic field" – six scholarships and 95% Common Entrance pass rate.

1981 saw the rebuilding of the cupola – a major triumph for A.L. Adams & Sons, who were the school's building firm for 25 years. It was removed and lowered to the ground where its legs and lead were replaced. The same year saw the arrival of the school's first computer, a Sinclair ZX81 and in 1983 the establishment of a computer room, with ten computers, caused great excitement.

In 1984 Mr Archdale decided to retire after 21 years, during which time he and his wife had not only overseen the move from Money Hill House to Redheath but had transformed the school into a thriving modern preparatory school. They were both so much a part of all that took place – and such a marvellous team. Mrs Archdale remembered over-hearing some boys, as Mr Archdale drove away up the

Arthur Joseph Archdale, Headmaster, 1963-1984

Above: The opening of the swimming pool in September 1987 by Old Yorkist His Honour Alan King-Hamilton Q.C., M.A.

Left: Father Christmas arrives at school, December 1987

Above: 1925 School Cricket Ist XI

Below: When opened in 1987 (see p.55), the school's swimming pool was considered to be ultra-modern

drive, saying, "Archie's out but look out, the Archess is still in"! "All their pupils and staff will be grateful to them and will look back on the Archdale years with affection and happy memories" – they were always very accessible, "little went on in the school without Mr Archdale's knowledge of it", and the individual boy was of paramount importance. During Mr Archdale's headship he developed excellent facilities and a "formidable academic record". He appointed specialist staff and led them by example – in 21 years, 48 scholarships were awarded. There had at that stage been only three Headmasters in 74 years!

Mr Archdale was succeeded by Mr Richard Robert Steel who with his wife brought "an injection of youth and style" to the school. He oversaw further major building developments – the magnificent indoor heated swimming pool (partly funded by appeal), the library and music rooms, the new side entrance and office. The kitchen and dining hall were refurbished (and the school rescued from imported meals by the appointment of contract caterers!).

In 1988 Mr White died and a moving memorial service was held in St Mary's Church, Rickmansworth. He was "a man of immense courage and determination which resulted in the school flourishing" and "his enthusiasm for History and Classics, and his handwriting...was an example to us all" during his 26 years as Headmaster of York House.

In 1990 Mr Steel moved to take over the headship of Wellesley House in Kent, after six years at York House, and was succeeded by Mr Patrick Brian Moore, formerly Headmaster of Glenhow in North Yorkshire for just over seven years. Fees were now £995 per term.

Right:
Richard Robert Steel,
Headmaster, 1984-1990

In 1991 York House achieved its best ever academic results, with six scholarships and 100% Common Entrance pass rate, following this in 1992 with another six scholarships and – in the new age of averages and league tables – the best ever set of Common Entrance average grades.

The early nineties saw the worst recession in Britain for decades and this, for a while, took its toll. Nonetheless the school's excellent reputation in the area and its magnificent site meant that, while building projects etc. were delayed, the school's future was never at risk. Academic results throughout the nineties were excellent and the school's avowed intention of producing "a thoroughly decent, all-round boy" was achieved, thanks to a dedicated staff whose enthusiasm enabled us to ensure that boys receive a broad and balanced curriculum, while at the same time being thoroughly prepared for their public examinations.

In 1993 Mr Bernard Ratcliffe retired after a remarkable 33 years on the Board, 26 of those as Chairman. He was succeeded by Mr Trevor Slade, also a past parent (and formerly Chairman of the Parents' Association) who had been on the Board since 1977.

In 1995 Mr David Davies retired after a magnificent 31 years' service to the school, during which time he had taught Latin to hundreds of boys and been a tower of strength, as Senior Master, in the daily administration of the school.

September 1995 also saw the start of a brave new venture. Mrs Wendy Wilson, having run a renowned Kindergarten at Northfield School in Watford, came to York House to start our Kindergarten, with 13 boys and girls (aged from 2 to 5 years), in the two downstairs classrooms in the main building. In the space of five years this grew to a total of 7 staff and 54 children and expanded into the Drawing Room, at which stage Mrs Wilson left to enjoy a richly-deserved retirement.

1997 saw the completion of Phase I of the York House Development Plan. This consisted of a splendid combined sports hall and theatre (to replace the 1966 Arnold White Hall); a new computer suite and a library adjacent to it (named the Arnold White Library) and a new Headmaster's residence (an extension to, and refurbishment of, part of the Tudor stable block). The old library was refurbished and transformed into an excellent Music studio. Unfortunately Mr Archdale was not well enough to attend the opening of the Archdale Hall (although he had been kept fully informed of its progress by means of plans and photographs), so it was opened on his behalf by his son, Nigel, Headmaster of Cheltenham College Junior School. His two daughters attended and Mrs Archdale later visited the building, which has a large stage, a sports floor area of two badminton courts and is well-equipped for indoor PE and sports activities as well as for music and drama.

In April 1999 Mr Archdale died in Brockenhurst, in the New Forest, to which village he had retired. His family decided that they would not have a Memorial Service at York House, Mrs Archdale saying "The Archdale Hall will stand as a lasting memorial. Joe really appreciated the honour involved in its inception and dedication. I think, therefore, that it would be best if we just remember him through that". She was, however, pleased later in the year to know that Speech Day "had sensitively incorporated an appropriate ceremony to mark the end of Joe's life".

Speech Day 2000 was another memorable occasion. The Guest of Honour was Judge Alan King-Hamilton who started at York House in 1911. It was 70 years since he had first presented the prizes and 35 years since the second time he had done so! His address to us was witty, wise and moving.

As York House moved into the new Millennium, Phase II of the Development Plan was completed. In October 2002 we moved into a nine classroom combined Kindergarten and Pre-Prep. Building in the old kitchen garden at the back of the school. There were now almost 270 pupils and the main school fees were £2396 per term, up from £1876 in 2000.

Phase III was to see the demolition of the old "temporary" blocks, which had housed two junior classrooms, Science, Art and Design Technology. The new brick building was to provide state-of-the-art Science, Art and Design Technology rooms and a four classroom Junior Department.

This project was halfway towards completion by the summer of 2005 when Mr Patrick Moore retired from York House, where he had been Headmaster for fifteen years. His wife, Carol , had undertaken a variety of roles during this time – Headmaster's Wife, swimming coach, Pre-Prep Teaching Assistant and First Aid Supervisor. Mr Trevor Slade (then Chairman of Governors) said of Mr and Mrs Moore, "During

*Right:
Patrick Brian Moore,
Headmaster, 1990-2005*

those years they oversaw many changes, changes in personnel, the introduction of a Kindergarten and new building structures. From the beginning Mr Moore had a vision of what he wanted York House School to be. He set high standards and had high expectations. His approach to education was a traditional, disciplined one and he demanded, from both pupils and teachers alike, academic rigour". This approach saw many York House boys being awarded Scholarships to a variety of Public schools, as well as invariably gaining entrance to the senior school of their first choice. York House boys also gained in reputation for good manners, fairness and honesty.

September 2005 saw the arrival of only the sixth Headmaster in the school's entire hundred years' history, Mr Peter MacDougall, who had been Headmaster at Brentwood Preparatory School for seven years. His wife, Claire, also joined York House as Headmaster's Wife and School Matron.

The summer of 2008 saw the retirement of Mrs Kerry James after 21 years' loyal service to three Headmasters as Headmaster's Secretary. Up to this point in the school's history there had only been three secretaries since the move from Money Hill House to Redheath in 1966 – the others being Mrs Margaret Smith (Secretary and Bursar) and Mrs Shirley Hayzelden. Other examples of long service and loyalty shown by the staff are Miss Angela Palmer and Mr Tim Thomas, who are both still teaching at the

Above: Class work c.1960

Left: The Computer Suite in 2006

Peter Ramsay MacDougall, Headmaster since 2005

school after more than 30 years. Mrs Pamela Evans, Mr Malcolm Turnbull and Mr Philip Byford are all still serving York House School after over 20 years, while Mrs Claire Roffe, Mrs Penny Brown, Mrs Karen Dingley and Mr Chris Lewington have all been at York House for over 15 years.

In November 2008 Mr Trevor Slade retired as Chairman of Governors after 32 years on the Board, 16 of them as Chairman. He is succeeded by Mrs Gill Noach, like Mr Slade, a past Chairman of the Parents' Association.

September 2009 saw a major change at York House, under Mr MacDougall's leadership. For the first time in the school's history girl pupils (aged 4+) were accepted into Reception (having previously left at the end of Kindergarten) and so the first steps were taken towards becoming a fully co-educational establishment. Main school fees are now £3340 per term.

In March 2010 we were sorry to hear of the death of our oldest Old Yorkist, Judge Alan King-Hamilton (see pages 55 and 58), at the age of 105. He is the happy little boy on the extreme right of the front row in the school group of 1911 (see page 37).

Above: The School Choir c.1960;

Below: The School Big Band practising in 2006

AUTHOR'S NOTE

I apologise for any errors or omissions which may have occurred during the compilation of most of this book over the period 1995 - 2004, rather as a hobby than with a view to publication beyond the school, and also for the quality of some of the older photographs, particularly those for which original prints or negatives could not be found. I would wish to express my gratitude to Mrs Claire Roffe for all her help in finding additional illustrations for this version and to Mr John Norris for all his impressive work which has enabled the transformation of the third edition of my work into a formal publication in 2010.

The gates are the same but the beautiful building's use has changed since this lovely view was photographed - and the large conifers near the house were felled by the storm of 1990

REFERENCES and ACKNOWLEDGEMENTS

Mr and Mrs A.J. Archdale
Dr A. Booth
Mr W. Broughton
Mr P. Byford
Camden History Society Newsletter, No. 73/ Sept.1982, Mary Elsy
Mr A. Capper, OY
Mr J.H. Chaplin, OY
Mr A.V. Collins, OY
Cussans' *History of Hertfordshire*, Vol. III
Mr D.J.A. Davies
Deeds of sale of Redheath & adjacent properties, donated by Mr J. Pierson
Deeds of Oak Farm and Redheath, loaned by Mr J. Craddock
Dept. of Environment, 1985: List of buildings of special architectural and historical interest
English Heritage inspection report: Ms Gee and Dr Bowdler
English Heritage Monuments Record Office
Mrs M.F. Furmedge
Hertfordshire County Record Office
Historic Hertfordshire, R. Roberts
author/date unknown: *History of Watford*
R.C. Eliott: *Homes of History and Romance*
Judge A. King-Hamilton, OY
Mrs M.J. Jackman
Mrs J. Lamble
Lymington Times
The Owl magazine
R.A. Norris: *The Parish Church of St Peter, Berkhamsted*
Peninsular and Oriental Steam Navigation Company
N. Pevsner: *The buildings of England: Hertfordshire*, 1977
Preparatory Schools' Year Books
Mr C.B. Ratcliffe
Dr I. Reynolds
Mr G.H. Rice, OY
Rickmansworth Historian, Spring 1963 – F.I. Paddock
Rickmansworth Historian, 1965
Rickmansworth Historian, 1978 – G. & R. Naylor-Smith
Rickmansworth Historical Society
Mrs Roberts
Mr D. Roger Jones
Baroness Sharples (granddaughter of William Newell)
Mrs J.E. Sherwood
Mr T.J. Thomas
Mrs D. van-Canter
Victoria "History of the county of Hertford", 1908
A. Wigens: *A view into Hertfordshire*
Watford Observer
Mr D. White, OY
Mr S. Worley, OY
Mr H.C. Wraith, OY
The Yorkist magazine
Mrs M. Young

Contents

Who were the Greeks?

The works of Greek thinkers, writers and artists who lived a very long time ago are still admired today. Students study the Greeks' ideas about science and law. Builders copy the style of ancient Greek buildings. People enjoy the beauty of Greek poetry, statues and painted pottery. The influence of the ancient Greeks has spread all over the world.

△ The Greeks were the first to use elegant stone columns to support a roof. Many ruins like this temple have been found and preserved so that we can still look at Greek buildings.

The first Greeks

People first lived in Greece about 8000 years ago. They led a simple life, hunting and trying to grow enough food to live on. About 3000 years later a very different way of life began on an island off the coast of Greece, called Crete. There, people learned to build and paint and make beautiful objects. Their **civilization** is called Minoan, after Minos, their king. This was the beginning of the first civilization in Europe. The people on the island of Crete knew how to read and write, but their language was not Greek.

The first Greek-speaking people began to invade the Greek mainland from the north and east around 2000 BC. They learned from the Minoans and built palaces at sites like Mycenae. The Mycenaean

◁ Greek craftsmen made beautiful jewellery using silver, gold and precious stones thousands of years ago. Some of the styles are still copied today. Pictures on Greek vases show artists making bronze statues. Not many of these statues have survived. Over the years, people melted them down to use the metal to make new objects. We know what some Greek statues looked like because later artists made stone copies.

YOUNG RESEARCHER

THE GREEKS

Jacqueline Dineen

HEINEMANN

HEINEMANN CHILDREN'S REFERENCE
a division of Heinemann Educational Books Ltd
Halley Court, Jordan Hill, Oxford OX2 8EJ

OXFORD LONDON EDINBURGH
MELBOURNE SYDNEY AUCKLAND
MADRID ATHENS BOLOGNA
SINGAPORE IBADAN NAIROBI HARARE
GABORONE KINGSTON PORTSMOUTH NH(USA)

ISBN 0 431 00566 4

British Library Cataloguing in Publication Data
Dineen, Jacqueline
The Greeks
1. Greece, ancient period
I. Title II. Series
938

First published 1991

Designed by Julian Holland Publishing Ltd
Colour artwork by Martin Smillie
Picture research by Faith Perkins
Editorial planning by Jackie Gaff

Printed in Hong Kong

91 92 93 94 95 96 10 9 8 7 6 5 4 3 2 1

Photographic acknowledgements
The author and publishers wish to acknowledge, with thanks, the following photographic sources:
a = above b = below c =centre
Agora Excavations 1970, American School of Classical Studies at Athens p40*b*; Ancient Art and Architecture Collection pp7*a* and *b*, 11*a* and *b*, 16*a*, 17, 19*b*, 20*a* and *b*, 21*c* and *b*, 22, 27, 32*a*, 36, 37*b*, 46*a* and *b*, 56*b*; Bridgeman Art Library pp9 and cover, 58; C M Dixon pp4*a*, 6, 8, 13*a*, 21*b*, 23, 31*a*, 32*b*, 45*b*, 50*b* and cover; Ekdotike Athenon pp19*a*, 24, 25*a*, 34*a* and title page, 49, 55*a* and *b*; Robert Harding Photographic Library pp26, 38*a*, 43; Hirmer Fotoarchiv p31*b*; Michael Holford pp4*b*, 10, 12, 13*b*, 15*a* and *b*, 28, 29, 33, 37*a*, 39, 41*b*, 44, 50*a*, 51, 59*a* and *b*; Kunsthistorisches Museum, Vienna p56*a*; Mansell Collection pp14, 16*b*, 38*b*; Metropolitan Museum of Art, New York, Purchase 1947, Joseph Pulitzer Bequest p40*a*; National Bibliothek Osterreichische p25*b*; Picturepoint p34*b*; Planet Earth Pictures p45*a* (photograph Flip Schulke); Scala p41*a*.
The publishers have made every effort to trace the copyright holders, but if they have inadvertently overlooked any, they will be pleased to make the necessary arrangement at the first opportunity.

Note to the reader
In this book there are some words in the text which are printed in **bold** type. This shows that the word is listed in the glossary on page 62. The glossary gives a brief explanation of words which may be new to you.

civilization lasted 400 years. It ended in 1200 BC when more invaders came to Greece. Wars brought poverty. For nearly 400 years people had no money for buildings or time to make works of art. This period is called the Dark Ages.

Life began to change around 800 BC at the start of the Archaic period. Villages grew into towns, protected by hilltop fortresses. The people in each town and the nearby countryside lived as a group or small community called a **city-state.** By the beginning of the Classical period in 300 BC, Athens was the biggest city-state. During the next 200 years the brilliant talents of the Greeks reached a peak. Then came the Hellenistic period, when Greek learning and ideas spread to many other countries around the Mediterranean Sea.

▽ The Greeks do not call their country 'Greece' in their own language. Their word 'Hellas' now means the country of Greece. To the ancient Greeks, Hellas meant all the places with a Greek way of life.

How we know about the Greeks

Visitors to museums today can see objects made and used by the Greeks. By looking at these objects, we know the Greeks used coins to pay for goods. Farmers used tools of bronze and, later, iron. Greek children played with toys made of clay. Such objects have been dug out of the ground.

People who study the buried remains of ancient times are called **archaeologists.** Archaeologists have discovered the ruins of whole cities buried deep in the earth. They can see how people built their houses. They also find everyday objects like bits of pots and jewellery. All these finds help to build up a picture of the past and the way people lived.

Archaeologists have to decide where to look. They study what is already known about the history of an

▽ Archaeologists at work slowly uncovering evidence from the past. Soil is carefully scraped away. Weapons and other metal articles may have to be cleaned. Sometimes broken objects are put together again so that we can see what they looked like. If pieces are missing, skilled workers may make new copies. Every find helps to complete the jigsaw which tells us about how people lived in the past.

◁ When Heinrich Schliemann found this gold cup at Mycenae, it was bent and squashed. Archaeologists have pushed the cup back into its proper shape. The poet Homer described a cup like this, with birds on the top of the handles, in the *Iliad.*

area first. Sometimes they find clues in old books or maps. This was how the ruins of Mycenae were discovered. Mycenae was one of the hilltop **fortified** towns destroyed by invaders about 3200 years ago. The ruins of the fortresses were gradually buried, but people still told stories about the Mycenaeans. About 400 years later, the Greek poet, Homer, wrote two long poems about the Mycenaeans. One poem, the *Iliad,* tells of a long war and siege at Troy, a city which was captured by the Greeks. The other poem, the *Odyssey,* describes the wanderings of the Mycenaean hero, Odysseus, after the war. Homer also wrote that Agamemnon, the commander of the Greek soldiers, lived at Mycenae. A German businessman, Heinrich Schliemann, loved the *Iliad* and the *Odyssey.* He decided to look for the lost cities. He found the ruins of Troy in 1870 and Mycenae in 1876.

△ The picture in gold and silver on this bronze dagger shows men with shields and spears hunting lions. The dagger was found in Mycenae but the design is very like the work of Minoan artists. Archaeologists think artists from Crete came to work and teach in Mycenae.

Clues in words and pictures

Heinrich Schliemann decided where to look for Troy and Mycenae by reading Homer's poems. Although Homer is the first Greek writer we know about, archaeologists have found much older pieces of writing but these are not books.

In 1900 Arthur Evans began digging at Cnossus, on the island of Crete. He found clay tablets with writing on them. There were two styles of writing but no one could read them. The two styles, or scripts, were called Linear A and Linear B. More tablets with

△ Mycenaeans carved the words on these clay tablets about 3400 years ago. This script is called Linear B. The tablets are palace records of payments and lists of jobs and goods.

The Greek alphabet

Capital letter	Small letter	Name	Sound
Α	α	alpha	a
Β	β	beta	b
Γ	γ	gamma	g
Δ	δ	delta	d
Ε	ϵ	epsilon	e (as in *bed*)
Ζ	ζ	zeta	z
Η	η	eta	e (as in *bay*)
Θ	θ	theta	th (as in *think*)
Ι	ι	iota	i
Κ	κ	kappa	k
Λ	λ	lambda	l
Μ	μ	mu	m
Ν	ν	nu	n
Ξ	ξ	xi	x
Ο	ο	omicron	o (as in *pot*)
Π	π	pi	p
Ρ	ρ	rho	rh, r
Σ	σ ς	sigma	s
Τ	τ	tau	t
Υ	υ	upsilon	u
Φ	φ	phi	ph
Χ	χ	chi	kh
Ψ	ψ	psi	ps
Ω	ω	omega	o (as in *dome*)

◁ Many letters in the alphabet we use today come from ancient Greek letters.

Linear B script were found in Greece in 1939. An English schoolboy, Michael Ventris, began studying Linear B. It took him over 10 years to work out the language. No one has yet learned to read the older Linear A, the language of the Minoans.

From 700 BC many official records were carved in stone. These tell us about Greek laws and how places were built. We can also learn a lot about Greek life from writers who lived after Homer. The thinker, or **philosopher**, Plato wrote about his own ideas and about his teacher, Socrates. The historian Herodotus tried to separate the facts of history from the stories people told. Many works by Greek writers have survived because their pupils wrote out copies. The original books and papers have now been lost. For hundreds of years new copies were made and passed on.

The Greeks painted pictures of their daily life on jars, cups, vases and bowls. Many buildings were decorated with stone carvings. These **sculptures** and paintings show us what people looked like and what they wore.

During the last century many archaeologists took their finds out of Greece. They believed they were saving them for the future. These things are now on display in museums in places like London and Paris, Berlin and New York. Some people believe that such finds belong in Greece.

△ Many paintings on Greek pottery show scenes from the stories in Homer's poems. They also show special events, such as festivals and details of daily life. These paintings tell us as much as words. It is surprising how many things are the same as the way people live today. This vase shows farmers collecting olives. Two men use sticks to shake the fruit from the tree onto a sheet spread on the ground. A third man picks up the fruit. Olives are still picked in this way on some Greek farms today.

The Greek civilizations

3000 BC	The start of the Minoan civilization on Crete
1600 BC	The Mycenaean civilization begins on the Greek mainland.
1200 BC	Dorian invaders destroy the Mycenaean civilization
1200-800 BC	The Dark Ages
800-500 BC	The Archaic Period
500-336 BC	The Classical Period
336-146 BC	The Hellenistic Period

Government and society

Greece was not a united country. It was a collection of city-states. Each city-state, or polis, was independent. At first each state was ruled by a king with a council of rich landowners, or nobles. By the end of the Dark Ages, these landowners had as much power as the king. This type of rule by a group of nobles was called an **aristocracy.** Sometimes an aristocracy was overthrown by a tyrant. Tyrants were people who took power when they had no right to it. Nobles and tyrants ruled with no written laws.

There were frequent struggles to change the form of government. By the beginning of the Classical period, some city-states were ruled by an **oligarchy.** In an oligarchy, the government was controlled by a few rich **citizens.** Other people had no share of power.

In about 500 BC, a new form of government was introduced in Athens. It was called *demokratia* which means government by the people. The English word **'democracy'** comes from this Greek word.

In Greek democracies, all citizens had a say in how the city-state was run. They could vote for people to run the city. The Greeks did not include women and slaves as citizens, so they were not allowed to vote.

◁ The Acropolis in Athens. The word 'acropolis' means 'high city'. The acropolis of a city was built as a fortress against invaders. It later became the place of worship, with a temple to the city's special god. The city and the countryside around it together formed a polis. This was an area with its own government.

◁ Once a year, members of the assembly had the chance to ostracize anyone they disapproved of. Each citizen who wanted to, scratched a name on a broken piece of pottery. All the pieces, called ostraka, were collected and counted. If there were more than 6000 votes, the person with the most votes aginst him was exiled for ten years. Several ostraka have been found by archaeologists. One of these shows the name Aristeides.

How democracy worked in Athens

Each Athenian citizen was a member of the assembly. The assembly met once a week and any citizen, rich or poor, could speak at these meetings. A council of 500 was chosen each year by drawing lots. The council decided what was to be discussed at the assemblies and council members also looked after the management, or **administration,** of the city. A lottery was also used to choose a board of ten generals who were responsible for the protection of Athens against invaders.

Writers such as Plato, Thucydides and Aristotle provide information about Greek government. Aristotle wrote a long work, *Politics,* in which he discussed democracy and methods of government.

◁ Every year citizens of Athens took their turn to be judges, public officials or council members. The judges gave their verdicts on quarrels between citizens using bronze voting discs. If the majority of discs had solid knobs, the person was judged innocent. However if the majority were hollow, the verdict was guilty.

Clothes and appearance

We know a great deal about Greek clothes and hairstyles from the literature of the time and from statues and paintings on pottery. The climate of Greece was dry with mild winters and very hot summers. People kept cool by wearing loose and simple clothes. Men and women both wore a tunic called a **chiton.** The men wore short tunics for work and long ones for special occasions. These formal tunics often left the right shoulder bare. The women wore ankle-length chitons. In cool weather they wore a shawl, or **himation.**

Tunics and cloaks were kept in place by ornate brooches and some women wore jewellery in their hair. Rich women dressed their hair around elaborate headdresses and bands. Fashions were always

◁ Men's formal robes were draped and fastened with a brooch. Sometimes they wore a cloak over the robe.

changing, but women could buy wigs in the new styles from the market. Writers joked about the elaborate new hairstyles women had to wear. Men had fashionable hairstyles as well. In Athens, the men visited the hairdresser as often as the women, and both men and women wore perfume. Some women wore simple forms of **cosmetics,** such as chalk to whiten their faces or berry juice to redden their lips.

Most Greek clothes were made of wool. Some people bought cloth dyed in bright colours for their clothes. In Athens, women could buy lighter cloth called **linen.** Linen is made from the fine stems of a plant. Some clothes had patterns embroidered on them.

Only the rich people in the cities could afford to buy all these luxuries. Most Greeks were poor farmers. They kept a few sheep and the women of the house dyed the wool and spun it into **yarn.** Then they wove it into cloth to make simple chitons and himations. Working men wore short brown tunics. Men and women went barefoot or wore leather sandals.

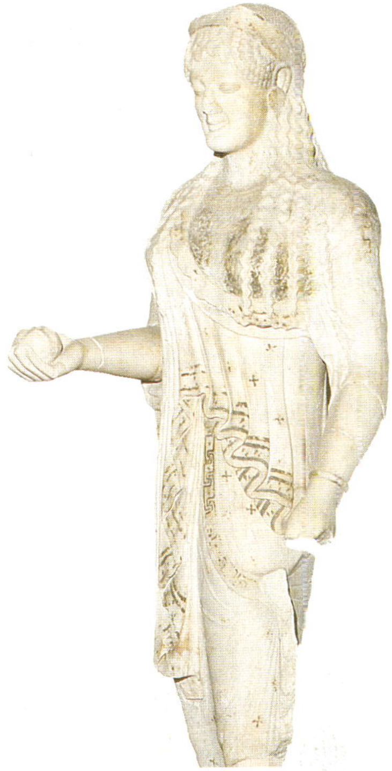

△ The chiton was a rectangle of material which was folded and fastened at the shoulders. This woman wears a himation over the chiton.

◁ All women except slaves wore their hair long. Some women let it fall in loose curls but most pinned or tied it into fashionable styles like the ones on this vase painting. They used wide ribbons or a hair net called a sakkos. By about 500 BC some Greek women were dyeing their hair. When they went out they wore a veil called a calyptra. This could be pulled down to hide the face, or put on the head as protection against the sun.

Family life

Plutarch wrote about the lives of Greek leaders in his best known books. The plays of Menander and Aristophanes describe the lives of ordinary people. Family life was important in Greece. People felt it was their duty to get married and have children. Marriages were arranged by the fathers of the couples. A husband and wife did not have to be fond of one another. A wife was chosen because she was suitable to be a mother. She was also expected to give money as a dowry to her husband. Sometimes the bride did not meet her new husband until the wedding **ceremony.**

Girls were normally married when they were about 15, but men were usually older. Plato thought that men should marry between the ages of 30 and 35. 'It is a crime to refuse to take a wife,' he wrote. Men over 35 years old who refused to get married could be fined or punished.

The wedding ceremony took place at home, not in a temple. The bride wore a white dress and a veil, like some brides today. On the wedding day, the

▽ Some Greek paintings show a chariot drawn by horses in the marriage procession. Only the richest families could afford a chariot. Most brides rode to their new home in a cart drawn by mules or oxen. The bride sat with her bridegroom, with his best friend behind. Friends followed on foot with presents.

bridegroom went to the bride's house with his friends. The bride's father announced to the bridegroom that he was giving his daughter to him. The girl then rode in a chariot or a cart with the man back to his house. He carried her across the **threshold** of the house. The bridegroom's family greeted the couple and led them to the hearth where a fire burned. The fire was a symbol of family life. The couple knelt by the fire and prayers were said. The next day, the bride's family came with presents, for a feast. The presents were usually painted bowls, cosmetics, boxes and oil jars.

A woman's life

Once a woman was married, she spent most of her time at home. She only went out with a maid, to shop in the market or perhaps to visit the hairdresser. Many wives had slaves and servants to work for them. In smaller houses, wives spent their time cooking and doing other household chores themselves.

A husband could divorce his wife at any time, but he had to give her back her dowry. She went home to her parents and the children stayed with the husband. Wives could divorce their husbands, but they had to give a reason in writing. A husband could also marry his wife off to someone else, without her agreement!

The naming of children

A new baby was named when it was ten days old. The Greeks did not have a family name. Sons were often named after their father or grandfather, and girls after their grandmother. Some children were named after a hero or god.

Relatives and friends were invited to the naming ceremony, or **amphidromia.** They brought small gifts and toys for the child.

△▽ Greek children played with hoops, balls and kites. They had toys made of pottery. Archaeologists have found many examples, like whipping tops and this doll. This baby-feeder has a spout which would be covered with a teat of cloth or leather.

Going to school

Children played at home until they were six or seven. Vase paintings and stone carvings show many scenes of mothers and children, and of children playing with toys. Children were often cared for by a nurse. Sometimes the nurse remained with the family for many years. In Homer's poem the *Odyssey,* the nurse is the only person in the household who recognizes Odysseus when he returns after 20 years.

Most boys went to school when they were seven. They were taken by a slave called a pedagogue who made sure they behaved properly. Girls did not go to school. They learned at home and helped their mothers with household tasks. Some families could not afford to send their children to school. The children had to help with work on the farm.

Plato wrote in detail about education in Athens. Education was divided into three sections: letters, music and athletics. These lessons are shown on many vase paintings. The boys learned to read, write

△ Teachers taught pupils to read from texts written on scrolls of papyrus. This was Egyptian paper made from a tall, thin plant. Scrolls were long sheets of paper, rolled-up. The texts would be written in ink. The pupils read the work of the poets, mainly Homer. They had to learn long passages by heart. In this vase painting a girl is reading from a scroll.

◁ Greek children learned to write on soft wax. The stylus scratched letters into the wax-coated surface of the writing tablet. Afterwards the wax could be smoothed over and the tablet was ready to use again. It is sometimes difficult to read Greek writing on pottery because words are spelt in different ways. The artists may have made mistakes because they were not taught well.

The Greek philosophers
Before the Classical period, civilizations had thought of brilliant inventions and made beautiful objects, but the people had simple beliefs. The Greek philosophers changed the way people thought because they questioned the traditional views of the world. They had firm ideas about the way people should think and behave, and they encouraged people to reason things out and to work out their own place in society. These men began the discussion and exchange of ideas which is the basis of learning today. The most famous philosopher was Socrates. His pupil, Plato, and Plato's pupil, Aristotle, left many writings about the philosophy of the Greeks. Plato and Aristotle both founded schools.

Socrates, 469-399 BC

Plato, 427-347 BC

Aristotle, 384-322 BC

and count. They wrote with a pointed stick, called a stylus, on tablets coated with wax. There were no desks, so the boys propped the tablets on their knees. They learned to count using the beads on an **abacus.**

Many vase paintings show music lessons. Both boys and girls learned to play stringed instruments and a type of flute. When boys were 14, they went to the *palaistra,* or wrestling school. There they were trained in wrestling, running, jumping, and throwing the javelin and the discus. A javelin is a light spear and a discus is a flat, round weight. This training was supposed to make boys strong enough to fight. Boys from wealthy families left the school when they were 18 and trained as soldiers for two years. Poor families only sent their sons to school for two years.

Many boys went to work with their fathers. Names on pieces of pottery show a father, his son, grandson and then great-grandson all worked in the same workshop. Xenophon describes how boys learned crafts as **apprentices.** Some young men continued to study with a philosopher. Aristophanes describes the school in Socrates' house in his play *Clouds.*

Living in Sparta

Life in Sparta was very different from life in the other city-states. Spartans disapproved of the thinkers and artists in other parts of Greece. In Sparta, the only important thing was to be a brave soldier.

Children became the property of the state as soon as they were born. All babies had to be shown to the leaders. If a baby was weak or ill, it was left to die. Children remained at home with their mothers until they were seven. Then the boys were sent to a boarding school. There they learned to obey orders without question. They learned to read and write, but training for war was more important. The boys were divided into groups. Each group had a chief, who taught the boys gymnastics. The boys were taught to accept hardship, hunger and pain. They slept in cold, uncomfortable rooms and were given very little food.

△ This bronze statue shows a Spartan warrior of about 500 BC. The warrior's hair is arranged neatly under his helmet. Herodotus wrote that Spartans combed their hair before battle 'that they might die with their heads tidy'.

◁ The founders of Sparta were Dorians who came from the north. They built their city on the banks of the Eurotas River in southern Greece. The plain was surrounded by mountains which protected Sparta from other invaders.

Life after school

All male citizens became soldiers when they left school. They had to give all their time to the city-state. They could marry but could not live with their wives until they were 30. They could not own their homes and had no luxuries. All this training made them the best soldiers in Greece, but their life was very harsh.

The history of Sparta explains why they led such a strict life. During the Dark Ages, warriors invaded an area called Laconia and fought the people who already lived there. These warriors set up an army camp, which became the city-state of Sparta.

They made the Laconian people work as slaves. The slaves were called helots, from the name of their village, Helos. There were many more helots than Spartans. The Spartans became such excellent soldiers because they were always afraid that the helots would revolt.

The Spartan government was an oligarchy. Only a few people could make important decisions. These were the 28 members of the Council of Elders. The Spartans elected two kings. One king led the army and the other was the chief priest.

△ Even the girls were trained to fight. The statuette shows a Spartan girl. She was probably an athlete. Spartan women led very different lives from women in the rest of Greece. They learnt to jump, run, wrestle, and to throw the discus and the javelin. This training made them strong and muscular. The Spartans wanted strong mothers for their sons. Spartan girls wore short, sleeveless tunics. Other Greeks were shocked by these clothes. They thought women's clothes should cover more of their bodies.

The gods of Olympus

Religion was important to the Greeks and like many of the ancient civilizations, they believed in many gods. Thales, the earliest Greek philosopher we know of, said 'all things are full of gods'.

People had many different ideas about the gods. Homer describes gods who looked and behaved like humans. Hesiod wrote a history of the gods and explained how Zeus used thunder and lightning to conquer rival gods. Thunder and lightning were thought to be signs of Zeus's anger. The philosopher, Xenophanes, thought there was only one god, who was not at all like a human. Another philosopher, Protagoras, was not sure that the gods existed at all.

Greek children heard stories, or **myths,** about the gods before they went to school. The 12 most important gods were said to live on Mount Olympus in north-east Greece. Stories about these Olympian gods and heroes such as Herakles, were told for thousands of years.

△ Herodotus and other writers explain why Athens was named after the goddess Athena. She found a baby and looked after him. He later became a king. He started the worship of Athena in his city and gave the city its name. This silver coin made in Athens about 470 BC shows an owl which was the symbol of Athena. The people of Athens believed their patron goddess would protect their city.

◁ Mount Olympus is the highest mountain in Greece, rising to 2917 metres. The ancient Greeks thought of Mount Olympus as the home of the gods.

The twelve Olympian gods

Zeus: the chief of the gods. God of the sky, storms, thunder and lightning. He married other goddesses, apart from Hera.

Hera: the wife of Zeus. Goddess of marriage and childbirth.

Poseidon: Zeus's brother and god of the sea. He used his trident to cause rough seas and earthquakes.

Demeter: goddess of farming and crops from the earth, especially grain. She was sister of Zeus and Poseidon.

Apollo: the god of light, thought, poetry and music. He was a son of Zeus and Leto. People thought Apollo could tell them about the future.

Artemis: Apollo's twin sister and the goddess of hunting and wild animals.

Ares: Zeus and Hera's son, the god of war.

Aphrodite: the goddess of love and beauty. No one knew who her parents were.

Hermes: the son of Zeus and Maia. He was the messenger of the gods who took the souls of dead people to the Underworld, a place with no sun in the centre of the Earth.

Hephaistos: Zeus and Hera's crippled son. As the blacksmith god, he made thrones for all the gods and goddesses.

Athena: the goddess of wisdom and war. She protected cities and arts and crafts. Athena taught Hephaistos how to use his tools.

Hestia: the goddess of the hearth and the home. She was Zeus's eldest sister and hated quarrels. One day Zeus announced his son **Dionysos,** the god of wine must have a seat on Olympus. Hestia gave up her place so there would not be an unlucky 13 gods and goddesses.

Apollo, the god of music, holding a lyre.

Artemis, the goddess of hunting.

Athena, the goddess of war, with her helmet and spear.

Temples and shrines

The Greeks spoke to their gods with prayers, gifts, songs and festivals. People prayed to the god who could help them most. Family houses had an altar in the courtyard. Vase paintings show soldiers pouring wine into a bowl on the altar or onto the ground before leaving home. They were asking the gods to keep them safe and for victory in battle. Plato said all wise men should pray every morning and night.

There were temples all over Greece for the many gods and goddesses. Each temple had a priest or priestess who performed special ceremonies. People did not worship inside the temple, so the temple had to look very grand from the outside. The temple was built as a home for the god. The image of the god, or the **shrine,** was inside. People left gifts

△ People believed that the gods liked rich and sparkling gifts. This golden bowl is decorated with three circles of acorns and one row of beechnuts. There are bees between the acorns in the outer row.

◁ The first temple of Apollo at Delphi was wooden and burned down by accident. Aeschylus, Pindar and Euripides all described the splendid new stone temple, built just before 500 BC. That building was damaged in 373 BC but rebuilt after a few years. The Greek travel writer, Pausanias, visited and wrote about Delphi 500 years later. Archaeologists began work 50 years ago. From the stones and from the descriptions of the ancient Greek writers they know what the temple once looked like. They have put back some pillars.

inside. Then they prayed at the altar in the open air. If they wanted a special favour, such as a good harvest, they killed an animal as an offering. They also made offerings if they thought the gods were angry. Each city had a special festival once a year. This was a ceremony for the god who protected the city.

If people wanted advice, they went to an **oracle.** This was a shrine with a priest or priestess who had special powers. People wrote their questions for the gods on lead tablets. The gods replied through the voice of the priest or priestess. The most famous oracle was at the Temple of Apollo at Delphi. King Croesus of Lydia went to Delphi and asked the oracle whether he should fight the Persians. The oracle replied that if he did, a great kingdom would be destroyed. Unfortunately for Croesus, this meant his own kingdom, and not the Persians!

Medicine and healing

When people were ill, they visited one of the Temples of Asclepius, the god of healing. A story said that a snake taught Asclepius, son of Apollo, how to heal. The first doctors in Greece were the priests in these temples. The secret remedies they used to cure patients were passed down from father to son.

The treatments consisted of bathing, fasting, rest and simple foods. People who were cured had their names and details of the cure carved on stone blocks in the temples. One of the most famous shrines to Asclepius is at Epidaurus. Many carvings about cures have been found there.

During the Classical period, a man called Hippocrates changed the Greeks' ideas about medicine. He did not rely on a god. Instead, he examined the patient himself to find out what was wrong and how the illness should be treated. Hippocrates founded a school of medicine on the Greek island of Cos, where he was born. Doctors had

◁ This stone picture was made as thanks for a cure. It shows what happened to the sick man. He went to the temple and made an offering to Asclepius. Then he slept in a room by the temple. On the right you can see Asclepius appearing to the patient in a dream and telling him how he should be cured. The snake leaning over the bed is the symbol of Asclepius. People thought that if the snake of Asclepius licked the eyes, it could cure blindness. In the morning, the patient repeated the dream to the priest, who then treated him. The snake is still the symbol of medicine today.

to take the **Hippocratic Oath** which listed their duties and how these should be carried out. Doctors still take this oath today. Hippocrates wrote about his work. Another doctor, Soranus, wrote a Life of Hippocrates about 500 years later.

About 100 years after Hippocrates, Herophilus founded a school of medicine in the Greek city of Alexandria. He was the first person to cut up human bodies and write about the insides. He taught doctors about **surgery.** Greek writing on stone tablets shows that doctors studied **herbalism** as well. One stone describes how a herb can cure soreness and scratches.

Patients could go to hospitals in Greek cities for free treatment. Xenophon writes of doctors who 'from morning to evening go and see their patients'. Patients had to pay doctors who visited them at home.

△ In this stone picture a man is offering a huge model of a leg as thanks for a cure to his leg. Archaeologists have found many models and stone pictures which have been offered by the ancient Greeks to their gods.

◁ A page from *De Materia Medica* of Dioskorides. He was a Greek doctor in the Roman army 2000 years ago. This drawing was probably copied from real flowers. The book was bought in Constantinople 400 years ago and kept in a library in Vienna. That is how we can trace herbalism back to the ancient Greeks.

Farming the land

Farming in Greece is not easy. The Greek climate is hot and dry and the landscape is mountainous with thin soil. Between the mountains are small valleys with richer soil. The farmer has to choose crops which will grow best in these conditions.

In ancient Greece, farmers grew wheat, barley, fruit and vegetables in the valleys. Herds of goats and sheep grazed on the dry mountainsides. The animals were kept for their skins, wool and milk. Vines grew on the **terraces** which were cut like steps out of the hillside. Olives were the most valuable crops. Not only did the trees grow well in the poor soil but the oil obtained from their fruit was used for cooking and lighting. The trees also gave shade from the sun. Vase paintings show farmers at work and the crops they grew.

The farmer's life was not very secure. Hesiod tells us about the life of a small landowner in *Works and*

▽ The Greek farmer of today has the same problems as the farmer in ancient Greece. The countryside and the weather are still the same and the work on a small farm is not very different. Farmers keep donkeys, sheep and goats. They grow vines on the terraced hillsides. They pick the grapes in August and make wine. Farmers in the valleys plant wheat and barley in the autumn. Crops are harvested in May. Greek farmers have always grown enough olives to sell to other countries.

When food was short in Athens in 591 BC, the leader, Solon, made a law. Farmers could only sell their crops in Athens. The law did not include olives because the farmers grew so many.

The Greek months

Gamelion	January-February
Anthesterion	February-March
Elaphebolion	March-April
Munychion	April-May
Thargelion	May-June
Skirophorion	June-July
Hecatombaion	July-August
Metageitnion	August-September
Boedromion	September-October
Ryanopsion	October-November
Maimacterion	November-December
Poseidaion	December-January

Days. He describes the farmer's year and his worries that the crops will fail. Landowners with small farms farmed the land themselves, with the help of slaves. If there was a bad harvest, the poorer farmers could not survive. They would become slaves. Some landowners were very rich. They employed **tenant farmers** to work the land. Xenophon describes an estate run by a rich landowner in his *Economica.*

◁ Scenes from everyday life were used to decorate walls and floors. This tiled floor shows a man ploughing.

The Greek city

The old cities of ancient Greece were built over many years. Tiny streets twisted and turned, and buildings were cramped together. The Greeks of the Classical period loved order. When they could afford it, they rebuilt parts of their cities. Streets were laid out to make the pattern of a grid. The streets were straight and crossed each other at right-angles. Buildings were arranged in neat, straight lines.

Wealthy citizens were proud to pay for new public buildings. Herodus Atticus gave money for a new theatre in Athens. Most cities had a market place, or *agora,* in the centre. Around the sides of the agora ran a covered arcade called a *stoa* where people could meet and talk protected from the sun and rain.

New cities were designed by town planners such as Hippodamus of Miletus. Aristotle wrote that, 'Hippodamus was a man who invented the planning of

△ The stoa in Athens has been rebuilt. The American School in Athens began work on the site about 50 years ago. The houses that had been built over the ruins of the stoa were knocked down. Nearly 5000 people were moved to new homes before work could begin.

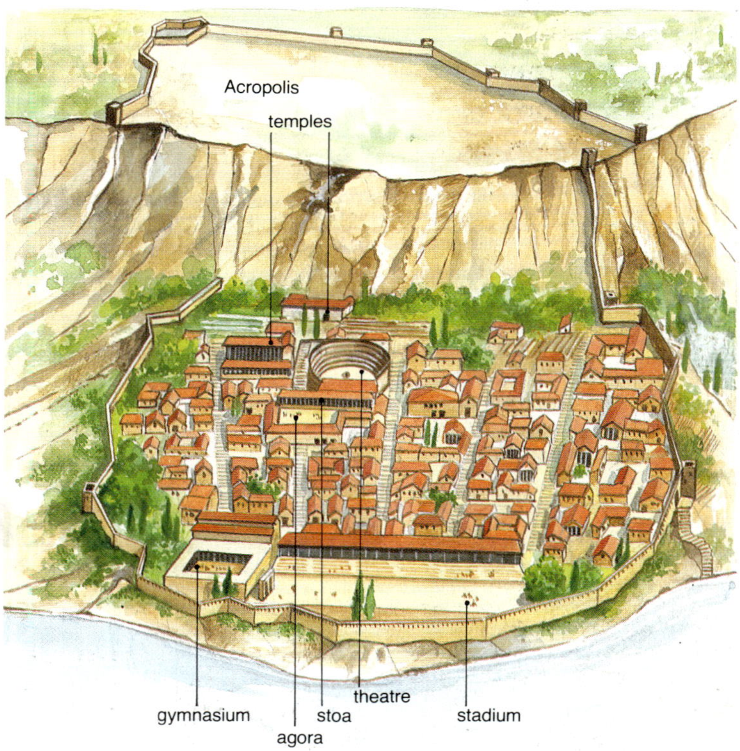

◁ Archaeologists have uncovered the city of Priene, on the west coast of Asia. Priene is one of the finest examples of the grid system. The city was built on a hillside. At the top of the cliff stood the Acropolis. Below were temples and a theatre for 5000 people. The steepest city streets were built like stairways. There were blocks of four or six houses along the streets. In the centre of the city was the agora and the stoa. There was a gymnasium where athletes could train and a stadium for athletic competitions lower down the hill. The city was surrounded by a strong wall.

◁ The Greeks loved beauty. They used stone columns for most of their public buildings and temples. There were two main styles of architecture, the Doric and the Ionic. Doric columns, first used between 700 and 600 BC were thicker and stronger. They had a plain, square stone slab at the top. The Ionic style used from about 500 BC, was more graceful, with tall, slim columns. The top of the column, the capital, was decorated with carvings like a scroll. The Corinthian style developed from the Ionic style in about 400 BC. The capitals were larger and carved like the leaves of a plant, called acanthus.

towns in separate parts. He laid out the Piraeus with regular roads'. Piraeus was the harbour area of Athens. It was built in 450 BC with straight streets on a grid system. The streets formed blocks for houses and separate blocks for public buildings.

◁ The Greeks began to use stone instead of wood, for their public buildings after 700 BC. Blocks of marble or limestone were cut from quarries. Then men carved the stone into shape. Columns were made by standing one piece of stone on top of another. They were held together by wooden pegs in the centre of each piece. Clamps made of iron or bronze held stone walls together. We know from Greek writers that pulleys were used to lift the stones into place. We can see metal clamps and the holes for pegs in the ruins of Greek buildings.

A Greek home

The Greeks built their fine public buildings of stone and marble, but their homes were built of sun-dried mud bricks. These bricks were cheap to make and easy to build with, but they crumble after many years. House walls were built on a firm layer, or

▽ Archaeologists believe a comfortable house at Olynthos looked like this. Drains from the bathroom and kitchen led to the street. Most rooms had windows onto the cool inner courtyard. The windows did not have glass in them. The women's rooms were at the back. They sometimes had their own sitting room on an upper floor. There was a room for slaves. The dining room was for the men.

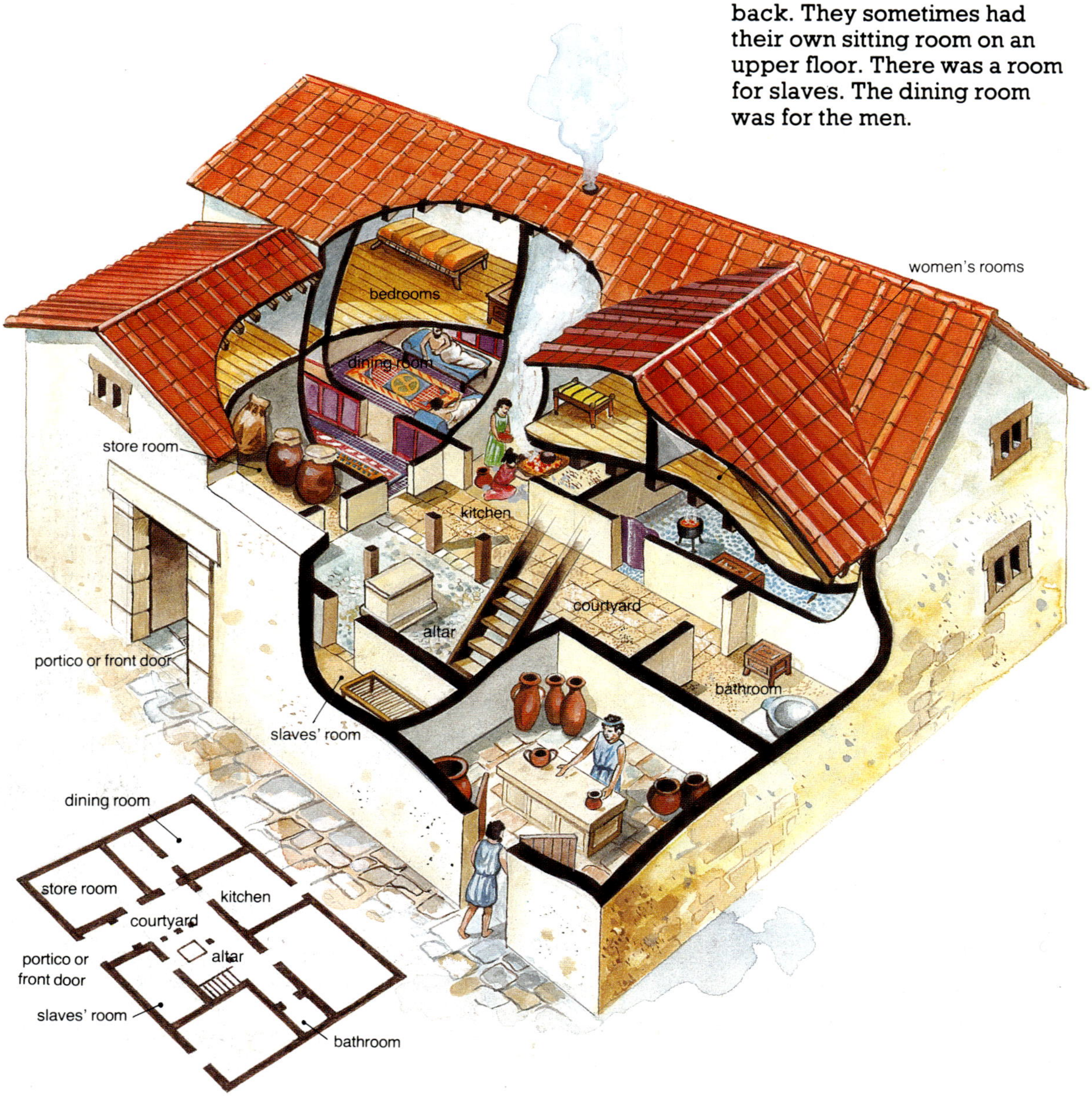

◁ This wall painting shows men at a feast. They are lying on couches and have low tables in front of them. In their hands they are holding their drinking bowls.

foundation of stone, and larger houses had stone floors. In the cities, the stone from ruined houses was often re-used for other buildings. About 100 houses of richer people have been found at Olynthos in northern Greece. People left the ruined city after a battle in 348 BC. No one lived there again so the stones remained. Archaeologists from the American School of Classical Studies began digging at Olynthos in 1928. They found stone floors and items like pottery, bronze mirrors and tools. These finds tell us what the houses looked like and what people did in the different rooms.

Furniture and decoration

Greek pictures show men lying on couches to eat. Dishes were put on low tables next to them. Furniture was made of wood so it has not survived. Stone floors kept houses cool. There were no carpets. Some houses at Olynthos had patterned floors of pebble **mosaics**. Rooms were lit with small olive oil lamps and heated with pans of hot charcoal. Some houses had a bath just big enough to sit in but most people poured water from a jug into a big bowl in order to wash.

△ From this stone carving we know the Greeks kept clothes and blankets in chests. Other articles were hung on the wall. Behind this woman you can see her workbasket, a round mirror, an oil jug and a cup. There is also a chair behind her.

Cooking and eating

In many households, the work in the kitchen was done by female slaves. They ground grain of wheat or barley to make flour. In parts of Greece today, women pound grain in the same way. This makes coarse flour and bread. Food was cooked over an open fire or in an oven made of pottery. Ovens could be carried outside. This kept the kitchen free of smoke.

Rich city people could buy food. Farmers grew their own food and sold some to the cities. Farming families made bread and ate it with goat's cheese, eggs, and vegetables. Fig trees provided fruit. All the Greek city-states were near the sea. The Greeks ate a lot of fish, which they sometimes dried for use when bad weather made fishing impossible. Farmers did not have enough good land to keep animals for meat so it was only eaten on special or feast days. Families kept bees and sweetened their food with honey. They made wine, and crushed olives for oil.

The main meal was in the evening. Guests were often invited to dinner. Women only ate dinner with the men if it was a party. A Roman, Cornelius Neppos, who visited Greece, wrote that he found this very odd.

During the Classical period, people began to eat more complicated dishes. This food took longer to prepare and cook. Larger households had a cook. The character of a cook often appears in Greek plays of the time. Several cooks might be hired to prepare a big feast. These meals had four or five courses.

Music and entertainment

A feast was normally followed by some type of entertainment. Sometimes there was a **symposium** during which guests took it in turns to speak on a given subject. They often spoke against a background of music.

In a work called *The Banquet,* Xenophon

△ All the water needed by the household either for washing or cooking had to be collected from the fountain. This job was usually done by slaves.

△ Many pottery models like this have been found in tombs. They date from 400 BC. They may show the life of the dead person or they may have been toys. This woman is cooking over an open fire. She is using a fan to keep the fire at the right temperature.

describes a symposium which Socrates attended. There were musicians, a dancing-girl and a jester. The girl turned somersaults through hoops fitted with swords. Plato's famous book, *Symposium,* records a talk given by Socrates.

The musicians played two types of stringed instruments. One was a type of lyre, the other was called a cithara. These were the most popular instruments. They also played a pair of pipes called an **auloi.** We know what these instruments look like from vase paintings. Also, an archaeologist found wooden auloi and bronze cymbals in Athens. Aristoxenus, a pupil of Aristotle, wrote about how to put musical notes on paper. Unfortunately, only a few fragments of written music have been found. We can only guess what Greek music sounded like.

◁ This painting on a wine jar dates from about 440 BC. The woman in the centre plays a type of harp. Above her is a cithara. On the left, another woman holds a pair of auloi. On the right, a young man holds a lyre. Writers of the time tell us that music was used in many ways in Classical Greece. Poetry was chanted to music. There were happy songs to celebrate events such as the birth of a child. Sad songs, or laments, told of a death. There were working songs and love songs. Dancing to music was a part of most Greek celebrations. As with the songs, there were dances for happy and sad occasions. Vase paintings show us the type of movements used in Greek dancing. They were full of rhythm and expression

At the theatre

Drama was a popular form of entertainment in Classical times. Every large city in Greece had a theatre. Plays were performed on 10 days each year. People crowded into huge open-air theatres to watch. It cost two **obols** to get in, but poor people could get the money from the city-state. The best seats were kept for important citizens such as priests and judges. The audience stayed for the whole day and watched several plays. During the intervals, they ate the food they had brought with them.

Greek theatre was different from modern theatre because it was part of a religious festival. The earliest form of theatre was a festival of songs and dances which was performed in Athens in honour of Dionysus, the god of wine. The songs were sung by a chorus. Speaking parts were introduced very gradually. At first, one or two actors stepped out of the chorus and spoke the main parts. This idea developed and by the Classical period, spoken plays were being performed. They were the first plays in the world. The plays were about the gods and heroes of legend so everyone knew the stories. They

△ The theatres were so large that the audience could not see the actors' faces clearly. Stone figures show actors wearing huge masks. There was a sad one for a tragic character and a happy one for a comic character. The masks of tragedy and comedy are still the symbol of the theatre today. There was also a mask for men who were playing women's parts.

◁ The open air theatre at Epidauros is still used every summer. The audience can sit on the same seats and see the same plays as Greek people did 2300 years ago.

enjoyed seeing how different writers told them. There were prizes for the best plays.

All the parts were played by men, because women were not allowed to act. There were only two or three actors in each play. They wore large masks to show what sort of character they were playing.

There were three types of plays. Tragedies were about solemn subjects. Comedies were about everyday things and made people laugh. A day at the theatre usually consisted of three tragedies or three comedies, followed by a short play called a satire. This type of play made fun of a serious legend. The most famous writers of tragedy were Aeschylus, Sophocles and Euripides. They wrote more than 300 plays, but only 33 survive today. The best-known comedy writer was Aristophanes, and we have 11 of his plays. People have admired the plays of these men ever since they were written and they are still studied and performed all over the world.

△ The architect Polykleitos designed the theatre at Epidauros about 350 BC. Pausanias wrote that it was the finest theatre in Greece. The theatre is shaped like half a circle. There is room for 14 000 people. The stone seats are built into the hillside so everyone can see. The theatre is designed so everyone can hear. The chorus danced and sang in the circular area called the *orchestra*. Behind that was the stage where the actors performed. At the back of the stage is the *skene*. This is a permanent background made of stone. Doors in the *skene* led to dressing rooms.

The games

Drama began as a way of honouring the gods. Athletic competitions began in the same way. Contests of strength were held at festivals for the gods. Gradually, they developed into organised 'games'. Competitions were held in running, jumping, throwing the discus and javelin, wrestling, riding and chariot racing.

There were several different festivals. The Isthmian Games were held near Corinth in honour of the sea-god Poseidon. The Pythian Games at Delphi were in honour of Apollo, and the Nemean Games at Nemea honoured Zeus. The most famous occasion of all, was the Olympic Games held at Olympia in honour of Zeus. The Olympic Games were banned by the Christian emperor Theodosius in AD 394 because they were held to worship a Greek god. They were not held again until a French sportsman Baron de Coubertin, organised the games at Athens in 1896. Since then, the Olympic Games have been held every four years, in different countries. The events are based on the contests held by the Greeks.

Olympia was not the same place as Mount Olympus, where the gods were supposed to live. It was a **sanctuary** to Zeus in southern Greece.

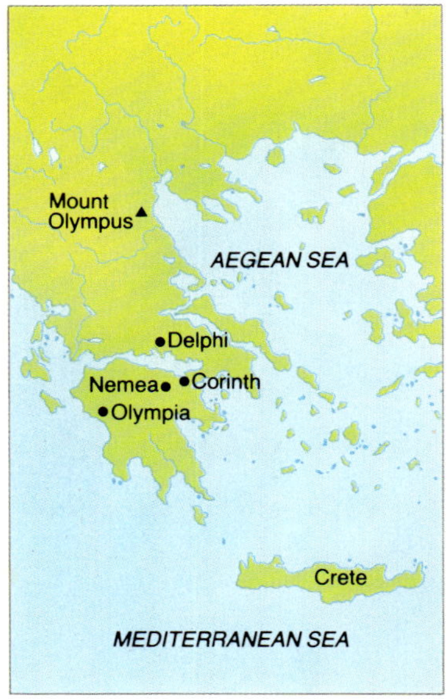

▽ Archaeologists from the German Institute worked on the stadium at Olympia from 1958 to 1962. It is one *stade*, or 180 metres, long.

◁ Vase paintings show us different events. Athletes always competed naked. There were separate running, wrestling and boxing competitions. The pentathlon consisted of five events: long jump, discus, javelin, running and wrestling. For the long jump, athletes held weights made of stone or metal. They jumped from a mound, swinging the weights which helped to carry them long distances. Some of these weights have survived. The picture on this vase shows a young man with jumping weights, or *halteres.*

△ Horse racing was a popular event for the spectators. Vase paintings and statues show us riders racing their horses at great speed. The main event of the Olympic Games was the chariot race. Chariots were drawn by four horses. Later, chariots drawn by two horses were introduced. Prizes went to the owners of the racehorses or the chariots, not to the drivers.

Archaeologists have uncovered the ruins of Olympia so we know exactly what it looked like.

The games took place every four years from 776 BC. They were held in June or July and lasted for five days. The date was announced by messengers who set out from Olympia and travelled all over Greece. The games began with a sacrifice to Zeus.

People came from all over Greece to watch or compete in the games. The athletes were not professionals but Greek men and boys who were very fit. Every city had a gymnasium where male citizens practised every day. Any men except slaves and foreigners could compete in the games. There were even events for children. Women were not allowed to take part. The winners received simple garlands of olive leaves. Their prize was simply the glory of winning. To win at Olympia meant life-long fame for the athlete.

Craftsmen and slaves

Most Greeks worked as farmers but in the cities some people had other jobs. The Greeks did not like to work for a master. They preferred to be self-employed because it made them more independent. Craftsmen set up their own small workshops to make the things townspeople needed. The council paid self-employed builders and craftsmen for their work on new public buildings.

Some houses had workshops where they made their own pottery. Other people bought from craftsmen. Every household needed pottery plates, bowls, cups and jars. Some children's toys were made of pottery. Craftsmen also made flat oil lamps from clay or metal.

Pottery for every day use was often painted. Some artists wrote their names on their work. A potter called Euphronios had a large workshop in Athens. He made cups and at first he painted them himself. Later, the names of ten different painters appeared on Euphronios's cups. Sometimes two artists worked on one painting. Some of these paintings show us other craftsmen at work and the tools they used.

There were carpenters who made wooden

◁ △ Cobblers made sandals and a type of boot with a pointed toe which men sometimes wore. In the picture on the left, a customer stands ready for the cobbler to draw around her feet so he can get the right shape for her sandals. In the picture above, the cobbler makes the sandal. Tools for shaping and sewing the shoes hang ready for use. Cobblers also used nails for the soles. Archaeologists discovered nails when they uncovered a shoe shop near the agora in Athens.

furniture and smiths who used metals such as iron and bronze to make ploughs, knives and armour. The smith's warm shop was a popular meeting place in winter. Basketmakers used reeds or willow to make baskets which were used for storing wool or as a container for fruit or grain. All these workers were men. Women only worked in the home. Fathers passed their skills to their sons.

Some Greeks did not have to work at all because they owned slaves. Slaves were always foreigners. They were often people who had been captured during a war and brought back to Greece. Rich families had several slaves and even the poorer farmers had slaves to help them. Slaves had no freedom. They were expected to do everything in the house. This gave Greek men the time to go to the assembly meetings and take part in the government of the city-state.

◁ Vase paintings show metal workers heating metals in a furnace. Metal workers made some household utensils such as knives and cooking pots. Ornaments such as buckles, and military equipment such as helmets were often made in bronze. Jewellery was made in silver or gold. Sometimes precious or semi-precious stones were included. Archaeologists have found earrings, bracelets, necklaces and rings.

The agora

To buy a pot or a basket, a Greek could go to the craftsman's workshop or to the agora. The agora was a large open space in the centre of most Greek cities. Around the agora there were temples, law courts and buildings where the assembly met. The word agora meant a meeting or assembly, before it became a market place as well. Some cities also had market buildings. In Athens there was a corn exchange, where merchants bought and sold grain. The city of Megara had a building where perfume was sold. Archaeologists have found many perfume bottles there, made of pottery.

The agora was divided into areas for different types of produce. They were all named 'cheese', 'wine', 'fish', and so on. The goods were laid out on stalls. Some sellers had small covered shops with roofs and walls of reeds.

Potters, bronze workers, and stone carvers had workshops on two sides of the agora in Athens. The craftsmen got plenty of customers because the market was busy. At the edge of the agora, groups of slaves waited to be hired for work or bought by new owners.

△ These men are using balance scales to weigh goods. Greek weights were called talents. One talent was nearly 26 kilograms. The historian Herodotus wrote that King Pheidon of Argos introduced a system of weights and measures to Greece about 650 BC.

◁ Archaeologists can often piece together enough information from ruins and the objects they find for artists to make detailed pictures of what a place may have looked like. This is what the agora in Athens may have looked like in Classical times. Pausanias wrote a detailed description when he visited the agora.

The bankers sat at counters on the agora, ready to lend money to people who needed it. They charged **interest** on the loan, just as banks do today. Each city-state had its own coins. Merchants often brought back coins from other city-states they had been visiting. They could change these coins into their own currency at the bankers' stalls.

Rich women only went to the agora if they wanted to buy something for themselves like perfume or jewellery. They did not shop for food or household goods. They did not even send a maid. The husband or his slave did the shopping. He chose the goods he wanted and then asked for them to be brought to his home. People did not have shopping bags. In his play *Lysistrata,* Aristophanes describes soldiers buying vegetable puree and carrying it in their helmets.

△ The fishmonger on this vase uses a large knife to cut pieces of fish for a customer. The fish stall was an important part of the agora. In the towns people bought fresh food every day.

Greek coins

At first, the Greeks traded by exchanging goods. They did not use money until 900 BC. Then they began to use thin rods of iron, called *obelos.* A handful or bundle of obelos was called a *drachma.* Coins were introduced about 650 BC. Each city-state had its own design. Many coins have been found and some of the pictures on them show us what the Greeks thought the gods looked like. This coin from Dodona shows Zeus. Some tell us more about the city. The coin of Mende shows Dionysus on one side and a vine on the other. Mende was famous for its wine. In Classical times there were two units of money, the obol and the drachma. Six obols were worth one drachma. There was very little gold in Greece. Most Greek coins were made of silver.

Colonization and trade

Archaeologists have found Greek coins and articles such as pottery in countries outside Greece. This evidence shows us that the Greeks traded with other countries. The Greeks also settled in other lands and built cities with buildings just like those in their homeland. The ruins of these buildings show us where the Greeks settled. These places were called **colonies.**

Between 800 and 700 BC, the population of Greece grew so fast that there was not enough land to grow food for everyone. The city-states sent people to find other land to farm. These people settled on land near the sea. They planted grain and vegetables to grow enough food for their own needs. Then they built new city-states. They had to be independent. They could not rely on help from the city-states they had left. As

▽ The Greeks founded colonies in Italy, Sicily, North Africa and Asia Minor. The map shows these colonies and the goods they traded. Few trees grow in Southern Greece or on the Greek islands. The city-states bought timber for shipbuilding from Macedonia to the north of Greece and from Sicily. Metal workers needed tin from Britain and copper from Cyprus and northern Italy to make bronze. Most of the grain from Egypt and Sicily went to Athens.

the colonies became more organized, the people began to trade. They sent anything they had a lot of, such as grain, timber, and metals, to other Greek cities. They bought goods they needed, such as pottery, oil and silver from Athens or wool and papyrus from North Africa.

The trading fleets

Businessmen, or traders, organized the movement of goods between the colonies and Greece. They also traded with other countries around the Mediterranean Sea, like Syria, Egypt and northern Italy.

Athens had a large fleet of merchant, or trading, ships. The ships were not owned by a big company. Each trader had his own ship which he sailed from April to September, buying and selling at different ports. From October to March the weather was bad and the seas too rough to sail. Many of the traders were foreigners who were not allowed to own land in Greece. They **invested** their money in goods to export. Sometimes groups of men shared their money in order to buy goods.

◁ The land on the Greek mainland and islands was not good for farming and there was not enough food for everyone. Greek painting, sculpture and architecture spread to other countries when Greeks travelled to found colonies. Ships carried goods and people between the islands, the mainland and other countries. The quickest way to travel was by sea.

Transport

Greece has a long coastline. The easiest way to travel was by ship, so most people lived near the sea. Ships kept close to land whenever possible. Greek sailors did not like to sail across open sea. When they had to, they steered by the sun or by watching the stars at night.

Many large pottery jars, called *amphorae,* have been found on wrecked Greek ships. These sealed jars were used to carry oil, grain and wine. They are evidence of the trade by sea between Greek cities. Merchant ships were big, wooden sailing ships. There was plenty of room for cargo, but the ships were slow. If the wind dropped, they could not move at all.

The merchant ships were often protected from pirates by warships called **triremes.** A trireme had oars as well as sails. It did not have to rely on the wind and could travel much faster than a merchant ship.

△ Greek paintings help archaeologists piece together parts of wrecked ships. This cup was made in Athens in about 500BC. It shows a heavy, wide merchant ship on the left and a long, narrow trireme on the right. Triremes were built for speed. They were about 35 metres long and 5 metres wide.

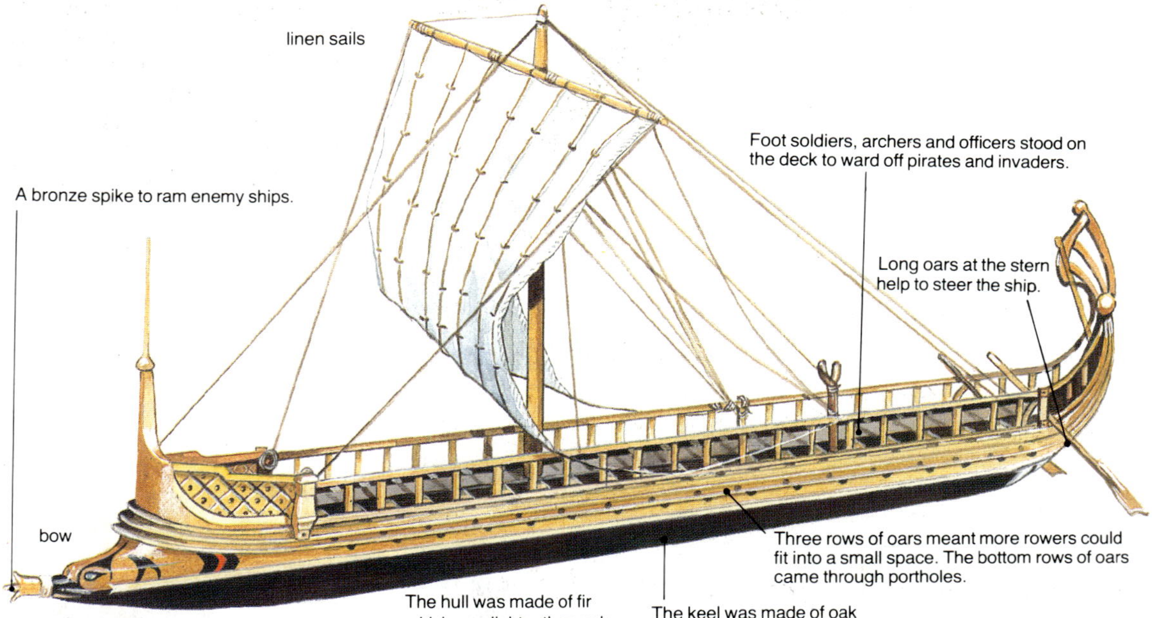

◁ Archaeologists work underwater as well as on land. They dive down to examine shipwrecks on the sea bed. They make notes and drawings and check whether the ship can be moved. As Greek ships were made of wood, they rotted in sea water. Sometimes pieces are found and brought to the surface where the wood is treated with preservative to stop it crumbling. Often other things are found, such as cargo, or utensils and weapons. This is another important way of finding out how people lived in the past.

Ships may sink because of storms or during battles. Underwater archaeologists study historical records to work out where ships have been lost. In the 1950s, a sunken ship was located off Artemesiun in Greece. The jockey in the picture was found in the wreckage. Years later more bronze pieces were found in the wreck by another diver. When the pieces were fitted together the archaeologists found that it was the rider's horse. So the horse and rider were reunited after 2200 years.

If people had to travel by land, they walked or rode on horseback. There were also two-wheeled chariots and carts, and larger four-wheeled carts for carrying several passengers and their luggage. Goods were also carried by cart, or in baskets on a donkey's back. There were no paved roads except to famous shrines, like those around Athens, and from Olympia to the sea coast. The risk of being robbed or killed by bandits made land travel even more unpopular.

Greek soldiers

Each city-state had its own army during the Classical period. Sparta had an army of full-time soldiers, but in the other city-states, young men trained as soldiers for two years when they left school. In Athens, they joined the *ephebes,* which was a military training group organised by the city-state. They were sent to country fortresses or camps on the coast. They guarded the borders of the city-state of Athens from invaders and learnt to be soldiers at the same time.

After this training, men were called up to join the army if there was a war. The main force of the army were the foot soldiers or hoplites. Hoplites had to buy their own helmet, sword, shield, breastplate, spear, and leg protectors called shinguards. People who could not afford this equipment became oarsmen on the triremes.

The hoplites fought in a **phalanx.** A phalanx was a square formation made up of 256 hoplites. Each soldier stood very close to the next man so that his body was partly protected by his neighbour's shield.

△ The Greeks had several styles of helmet. They were designed in different regions of Greece. The most successful was the Corinthian helmet like the example in the picture. The design did not change much for 300 years. This type of helmet protected the nose and cheeks as well as the head. Vase paintings often show plumes on Greek helmets.

◁ The painting on this bowl from the fifth century BC shows a hoplite in armour. He wears a short pleated tunic, and a helmet. He carries a shield and a spear. This soldier seems to have bare feet, but other paintings show hoplites wearing sandals.

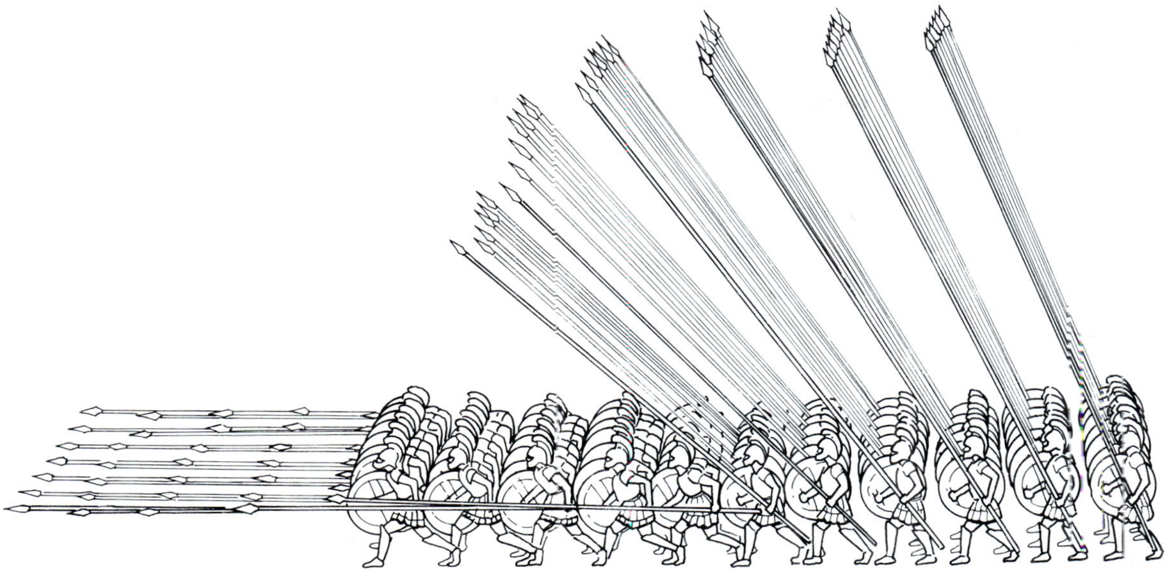

△ The long spears were an important part of the phalanx in action. The first five rows of hoplites held their spears out in front of them. They did not have to get too close to the enemy before striking them. Row after row of hoplites marched towards enemy soldiers, like a battering ram. If any enemy remained, the hoplites fought them with swords.

Peltasts armed with shields and spears were grouped on each side of the phalanx. Some armies had **cavalry** who rode on the outside of the whole group.

Phalanx fighting was very effective. First the peltasts threw spears at the enemy, then moved back behind the phalanx. The phalanx moved forward and forced the enemy soldiers to move apart. Hand-to-hand fighting followed while the peltasts and cavalry moved in on each side of the enemy and forced them to run away or be taken prisoner.

Greek armour

A good deal is known about Greek armour because metal lasts a long time and many examples have been found. The hoplite wore a bronze helmet and breastplate over a short tunic. He carried a bronze shield called a hopla. His legs were protected by shinguards or greaves which were also made of bronze. His weapons were a sword which was 70 centimetres long and a spear which was usually 2 to 3 metres long. The Theban army used spears which were 6 metres long.

War on land and at sea

City-states such as Athens and Sparta were great rivals and often fought each other. However, when a foreign army threatened Greece, the city-states could ask each other for help.

To the east of the Greek city-states, the vast Persian empire had become very powerful under King Darius. In 499 BC the Ionian city-states rebelled against Persian rule and Athens sent 20 ships of soldiers to help them. At first the Greeks were successful and they burned the important Persian city of Sardis. After the Athenian soldiers had gone home, the Ionian Greeks continued fighting until they were defeated in 493 BC. However, Darius wanted his revenge on the Athenians. In 490 BC, he sent an army to attack Athens. The Athenian army, led by general Miltiades, managed to defeat the strong Persian force at the Battle of Marathon. Afterwards an athlete called Pheidippedes ran from Marathon to Athens with the

▽ Cyrus the Great made Persia the biggest empire in the world. When he defeated King Croesus of Lydia in 546 BC, the Greek city-state in western Asia became part of the Persian empire. Although each city-state had its own ruler, the king of Persia ruled over his empire from his palaces at Babylon, Persepolis and Susa. The Persians were not harsh rulers, but the Greeks were indepedent people and they wanted their freedom.

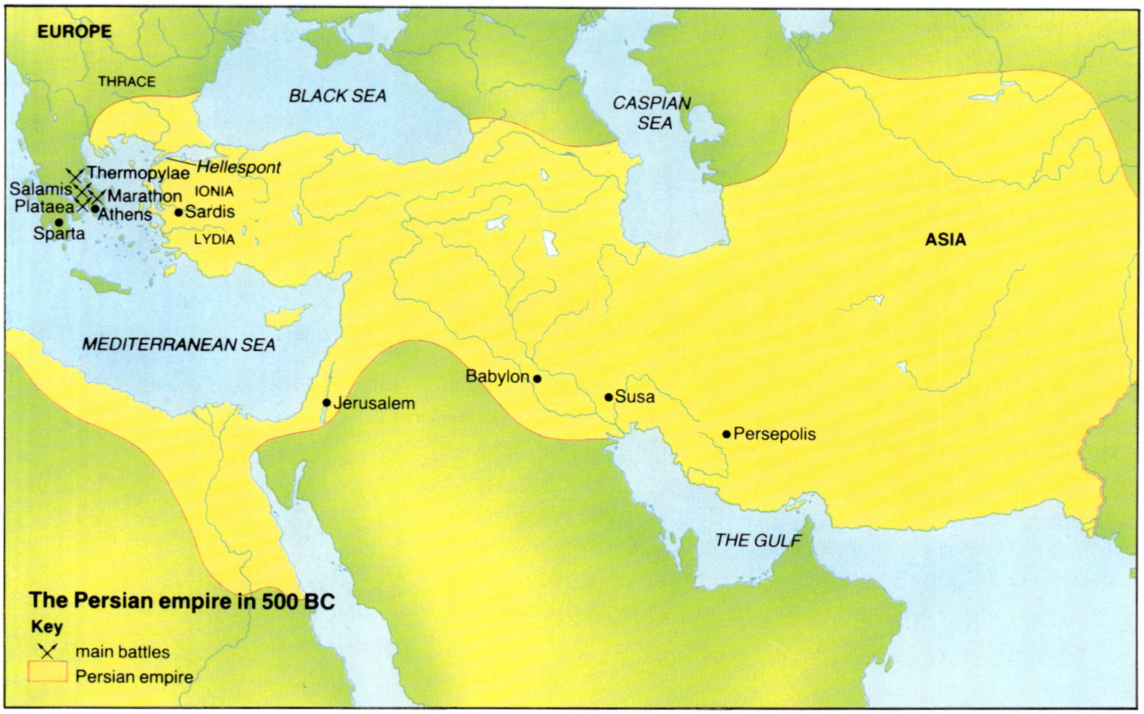

news. Marathon is about 40 kilometres from Athens. This is the distance of 'marathon' races that people run today.

Darius was furious at this defeat but he died before he could plan another war against the Greeks. His son, Xerxes, was determined to defeat the Greeks. The Athenian commander, Themistocles, persuaded the Greeks that they would only be safe from the Persians if they could defeat them at sea. The council agreed to spend the money to build a fleet of 200 triremes at Piraeus.

In 480 BC, after ten years training, Xerxes led his huge army into Greece. First they had to cross the Hellespont, the channel of water which divided Europe from Asia. In order to do this, the Persians tied 300 boats together to make a bridge.

The Spartans joined the war to help the Athenians, but their army was too small. Although the Greeks fought bravely, they were defeated at Thermopylae and the Persians marched on towards Athens.

△ After the Persian wars, the Athenians thought that Themistocles was too powerful and he was banished from Athens. People believe that this bust is a true portrait of Themistocles. It was made by a Roman artist but he copied it from a Greek sculpture which no longer exists. The Greek original probably dated from about 460 BC.

The battle of Salamis

Themistocles ordered everyone to leave Athens. The women and children went to the safety of the islands. The men joined the triremes to fight at sea. Themistocles planned to lure the Persian fleet to a narrow channel between the Greek mainland and the island of Salamis where it would be difficult for the Persians to move their ships.

The plan worked after Themistocles had sent a false message to Xerxes saying that the Greek fleet was trying to escape. Xerxes sent warships to block the Greek escape. The lighter Greek triremes were waiting to attack them. In the battle the Persians lost most of their ships, and the Persian army was finally defeated on land at the Battle of Plataea in 479 BC.

The Athenian empire

Although the Spartan army had defeated the Persians at the Battle of Plataea, it was the Athenians who grew in wealth and power afterwards.

The triremes Themistocles had originally needed before the Battle of Salamis had been paid for using silver from a mine at Laureion. The Laureion mountains were within the borders of the Athenian city-state. After their success at Salamis, the Athenians made their navy even larger. So although the Spartans still had the best army, the Athenians had the best navy.

However, the Greeks were still afraid of attacks by the Persians. The Athenians put forward the idea that the city-states should join together in a **league.** More than 200 city-states and islands joined. It was called the Delian League because its headquarters was on the island of Delos.

Each member of the league gave ships or money to build them. Using the ships contributed by the

△ Pericles was leader of Athens for 30 years, from 460 BC. He planned magnificent new buildings to make Athens the most beautiful city in the world. He said he wanted his city to be 'an education to Greece'.

◁ The buildings on the Acropolis in Athens had been destroyed by the Persians. The Parthenon was built as thanks to the gods for saving the people of Athens. An architect called Ictinus drew the plans for the temple to Athena.

The Parthenon
The sculptor Pheidias carved marble statues and scenes of Athenian life for the Parthenon, including a 12 metre high statue of Athena in gold and ivory. Over 500 painted statues stood around the temple. The carvings in the picture are part of the marble frieze which decorated the top of the temple.

league, the Athenian navy was able to destroy a new Persian fleet in 486 BC. The Athenian navy protected the other city-states and made them pay for this protection. Athens became more and more powerful. In 453 BC the Athenians moved the league's money to a treasury in Athens. They made all league members use Athenian coins. The league became an Athenian empire.

The people of Athens had money to spend on statues, paintings and beautiful buildings. They had time to read and write and discuss ideas. This was the time of great achievements in Greece – the Classical period.

The Peloponnesian war

Pericles' great achievement was to inspire the artists of Athens to create beautiful work. He wanted everyone to see the glory of Athens. He also wanted Athens to be powerful. Many Athenians dreamed of the day when Greece would become one state with Athens as the capital. The Athenian navy began to attack some city-states and force them to join the Athenian empire.

Sparta had never joined the Delian League because the Spartans did not agree with Athenian ideas. The smaller city-states asked Sparta to help them put an end to the wealth and power of Athens. Sparta joined with supporters in the south to form the

▽ This map shows how power was divided in the war. Sparta controlled the area called the Peloponnese in the south. Athens had supporters on the islands and in western Asia.

Lysander and Alcibiades
Two names appear in writings about the Peloponnesian war. Plato writes of Alcibiades, who was an Athenian. He wanted to be rich and famous and he hoped that the war would bring him power. It was his idea to attack Sicily, and this brought about the first downfall of the Athenian fleet. The fleet was finally defeated by a grim and cunning Spartan, the admiral Lysander, in 405 BC.

Peloponnesian League. They declared war on the Athenians in 431 BC.

The Peloponnesian war lasted for 27 years. Farms near Athens were ruined by constant fighting but the Spartans could not capture Athens. They could not storm the strong city walls which linked the city with the harbour at Piraeus. The Athenian navy attacked Sparta's supporters from the sea. Corinth had a trading navy but the Peloponnesian League did not have enough ships to defeat Athens at sea.

The battles went on until the Spartans agreed to accept help from the Persians. This gave them enough money to build a fleet. A Spartan general, Lysander, finally defeated the Athenian fleet by a surprise attack in the harbour at Aegospotami on the Hellespont.

Then Lysander sailed back to Piraeus. His ships stopped food getting to Athens. Starvation forced the city to surrender in 404 BC.

Aristophanes' play *Lysistrata* is about the Peloponnesian war. He shows that women wanted to end the wars. Many soldiers were killed and the women were left alone. 'Our only armour is our perfume, our dresses, our pretty little shoes,' they say in Aristophanes' play.

△ The historian Thucydides fought in the Peloponnesian war and felt bitter because Athens was taken over by Sparta. He wrote a detailed account of the war which is our main source of evidence. This bust of Thucydides was made many years after his death but people think this is what he really looked like.

△ A Greek woman says a sad farewell to her husband before he goes off to war.

The defeat of the city-states

The defeat of the Athenians by the Spartans brought changes to the city-states. The Spartans were harsh rulers who did not believe in democracy. So although the city-states were pleased to be freed from the powerful rule of the Athenian empire, they soon realised they were in a worse situation than before. The Spartans tried to rule the city-states themselves. Fighting broke out and in 371 BC the powerful Spartan army was beaten by a smaller army for the first time.

▽ Philip moved the capital of Macedonia to Pella. He became rich by taking over the gold and silver mines of his neighbours. He trained his men to be fierce soldiers and horsemen. Horses were expensive to feed, so cavalry soldiers were not common in the Greek city-states. This gave Philip an advantage.

General Epaminondas, from the city-state of Thebes, used a new idea. He formed his Theban soldiers into a crescent shape. When the Spartan army attacked, the Theban soldiers surrounded them. The Thebans put an end to Spartan rule.

△ This ivory head of Philip was found when archaeologists discovered the Macedonians royal tombs in Vergina in northern Greece.

Philip of Macedon

Macedonia was a wild mountainous area on the northern borders of Greece. The Macedonians did not all speak Greek. Their way of life was quite different from the city-states. They were ruled by a king. Philip II became king of Macedonia in 359 BC. He wanted to unite all the city-states of Greece under his rule and then seize lands from Persia. In 338 BC, Philip's huge army defeated the Greeks at a place called Chaeronea. The Greeks had to accept Philip as their leader. This was the end of democracy in Athens, but the city was still the centre of Greek **culture.** This was the age of the great philosophers. The works of Plato, Aristotle and Xenophanes tell us what the Greeks thought and talked about during this time.

◁ The tomb at Vergina was full of rich treasures. The tomb contained a golden crown, the gold arrow quiver on the left of the picture, silver bowls and cups and bronze armour. Writers who knew Philip say that he limped from a war wound. The pair of bronze greaves, to the right and centre in this picture, were found in the tomb. One greave was shorter than the other, so archaeologists think they probably belonged to Philip. The tomb itself is decorated with pictures of a lion hunt and there are other fine paintings.

Alexander the Great

When Philip was killed, Alexander said, 'Nothing has changed – except the name of the king'. Alexander was a brave and brilliant leader who had the same aims as his father. He had been taught by Aristotle who gave Alexander a love of Greek poetry and art and an interest in science. However, his main interest was in conquering other lands.

First of all, Alexander finally united the old city-states of Greece. Then he was ready to take revenge on Greece's old enemy, Persia. In 334 BC he marched into Asia. He defeated the king of Persia, Darius III, and brought all the lands of the Persian empire under Greek rule.

Alexander ruled over Greece, Persia and Egypt but he realised that people could revolt at any time and destroy his empire. To prevent this, he created Greek colonies in the conquered lands. The colonies were run by his own soldiers. Sixteen of the new colonies were called Alexandria. The city of Alexandria in Egypt became the centre of the Greek-speaking world.

Alexander treated the Persians carefully because they had once been the rulers of his empire. He suggested that his men should marry Persian women. He said they should think of all the world as home and all men as their brothers. The Greek soldiers did not like the idea. After all, the Persians had been their enemies for hundreds of years. So Alexander himself married a Persian woman, Roxane from Sogdiana.

After Alexander and his army had been on the march for 10 years, they reached India. Alexander wanted to cross this land which be believed marked the edge of the world. His soldiers, who had been away from their homes and families for a long time, wanted to return. On the way back Alexander caught a fever and died in Babylon in 323 BC.

Alexander was only 32 when he died and he had

△ This cameo of Alexander and his Persian wife Roxane, is carved in onyx. Alexander and Roxane had a young son. Roxane and her son were killed after Alexander's death. As he lay dying, he was asked who should rule after him. He whispered, 'The best'. No one could agree who the best was. His generals fought over the lands and finally, three generals divided the lands between them.

△ Alexander's influence spread far and wide through his empire and lasted long after his death. This elaborate temple was cut into sandstone at Petra, which is in Jordan. You can see the Greek style of columns and decorations.

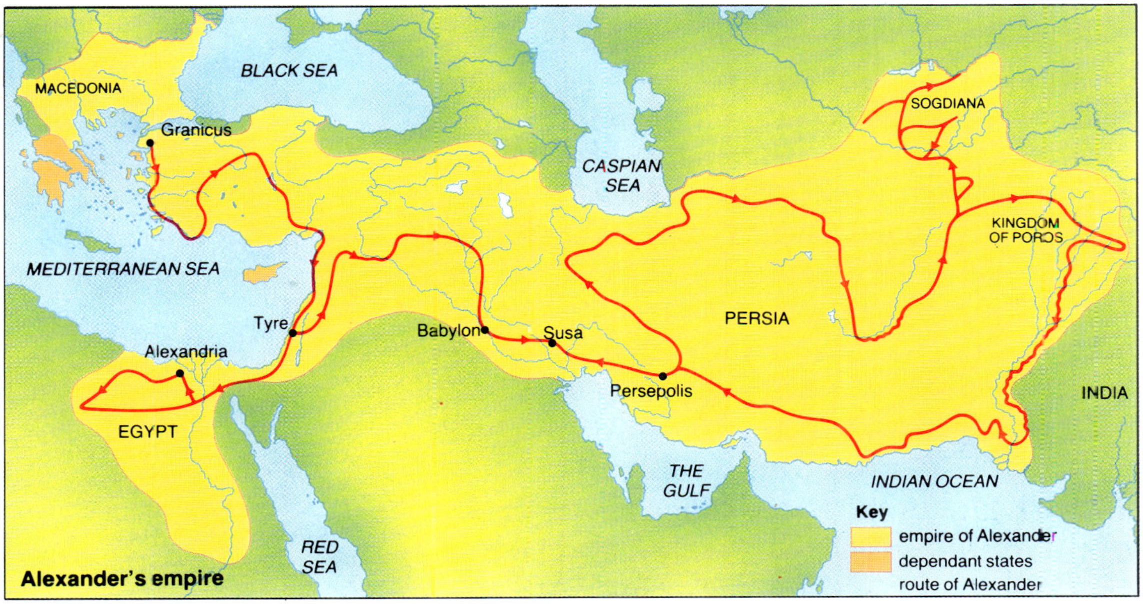

made no plans for his empire after his death. Eventually three of his generals took parts of the empire as kingdoms. Antigonus ruled Macedonia. Seleukos became king of most of Persia. Ptolemy took Egypt. Hellenistic culture and the Greek language dominated these lands for 300 years.

△ Alexander fought for 11 years to form his empire. He set out with an army of 30 000 foot soldiers and 5000 cavalry. They were Greeks and Macedonians. In 334 BC he defeated a Persian army at the Granicus River. Then he carried on south to defeat Tyre and Egypt. In 331 he captured the winter palace of the Persian kings at Babylon and went on to take their summer palace at Susa and the ceremonial palace at Persepolis. He spent three years defeating the eastern part of the Persian empire and marched into India. He defeated the Indian King Poros in 326 BC. Alexander's horse Bucephalus, died in the battle. Alexander wanted to go on to the Ganges River but his tired soldiers refused. Alexander agreed to turn back.

Science in the Hellenistic Period

The Hellenistic Period was famous for discoveries in science. Alexandria in Egypt was the main centre. Ptolemy I set up an institute for research called the Mouseion, or museum and library, next to his palace. It was a place where poets, scientists and scholars could study. There the mathematicians Euclid and Pythagoras worked out rules in geometry. Scholars studied medicine, machines, and the stars. The astronomer Aristarchus learned that the sun, and not the earth, is the centre of our universe. Eratosthenes worked out the distance around the earth, and he was very nearly correct. He saw that the sun at Assuan, in the south, was right overhead, or vertical, in midsummer. He then measured the shadow of a vertical pole at Alexandria in midsummer. He made his calculations from this angle.

The rise of Rome

The Romans had built a trading centre on the Tiber River in southern Italy. This later became the city of Rome. The Romans began to trade with the cities around the Mediterranean Sea. They were greedy for power. In 146 BC they conquered the wealthy city of Carthage in North Africa. Then they turned their attention to Greece. Mainland Greece was soon under Roman rule. The Greek historian Polybrus was taken to Rome as a captive by Aemilius Paulus. He wrote a *World History* to explain the rise of Rome to Greek readers.

After Alexander's death his empire gradually began to be taken over by Rome. First of all Macedonia was weakened by fighting with Greeks from the south. Then in 168 BC the kingdom was destroyed by a Roman army under Aemilius Paulus. The Roman general Pompey defeated the last Seleucid king of Syria in 65 BC. Cleopatra was the last of the Ptolemies in Egypt. The Roman Emperor Augustus took Egypt in 30 BC, and Cleopatra killed herself. The Romans had become powerful rulers.

◁ The Renaissance began as a study of Classical Greece but artists soon took on a style of their own. They were inspired by the work of the ancient Greeks but they did not copy them. The School of Athens shows how the Renaissance painter, Raphael, imagined the philosophers of ancient Greece.

The legacy of Greece

The Romans were fascinated by Greek culture. As Homer described it, 'Captive Greece made captive her rude conqueror'. They took Greek works of art to Rome and copied Greek styles of architecture. Young Romans went to Athens to learn from the philosophers and artists. Greek literature was copied by scholars and taken to Rome.

Rome was conquered by invaders in AD 476. Philosophy, art and literature were forgotten in western Europe for nearly 1000 years. Then, during the 14th century, scholars in Italy began to study Greek so that they could read Greek literature and philosophy. Painters and sculptors were again inspired by the art of Classical Greece. Wealthy Italians paid archaeologists to look for Greek statues and paintings. This was the start of the **Renaissance,** or rebirth of thought and art. The civilization of ancient Greece has influenced people ever since.

△ This pot was made at the factory of the English potter, Josiah Wedgwood, in about 1790. You can see that it is similar in style to the pots of ancient Greece but it is more elegant and delicate. The work of the Greeks still inspires artists and craftsmen to use their talents and create beautiful, original designs after thousands of years.

◁ The British Museum in London, England, was built in 1915. It has Ionic columns and carved decorations which are similar to those of ancient Greece. This shows how the Greek style has influenced architects all over the world.

Time line

BC

c 2000	First Greek-speaking peoples invade Greek mainland. Minoan civilization begins on Crete.
1600	Mycenaean civilization of Greece begins. Small, rich kingdoms flourish.
1200	The kingdoms of the Mycenaeans are threatened by the Dorians from the north.
1150	The Mycenaean kingdoms are destroyed. The Mycenaean age ends and the Dark Ages begin.
850-600	Homer writes his epic poems, the *Iliad* and the *Odyssey.* The Greeks adopt a new alphabet. Some people begin to leave their Greek homeland and set up colonies in the land around the Mediterranean Sea. The Dark Ages end and the Archaic period begins.
776	First Olympic Games held.
600-500	During the Archaic period many city-states are governed by oligarchies. The first Greek coins are made. By the end of this period democracy begins in Athens.
546	The Persians conquer Ionia as their empire spreads.
500	Archaic period ends. Classical period begins.
493	Ionian and Athenian supporters try to rebel against Persian rule, but are defeated.
490	Persians invade Greece and raid Athens. They are defeated at the Battle of Marathon.
480	Persian fleet defeated by Athenians at the Battle of Salamis.
479	Greeks defeat Persian armies at Plataea. End of Persian invasions.
477	Delian League set up between Athens and other Greek states.
449	Peace made with Persia. Athens begins to flourish under its new leader, Pericles, and the Parthenon is built.
431-404	The Peloponnesian Wars are fought between Athens and Sparta.
404	Athens surrenders to Sparta. The Spartan empire is created but the Spartans have difficulty controlling it.
371	Spartans defeated by Theban general, Epaminondas, at the Battle of Leuktra. Sparta's power is broken forever.
356	Philip II becomes king of Macedonia and his son Alexander the Great is born.

c 350 Philip tries to take over the city-states.

338 Philip defeats Athenian League at Battle of Chaeronea and dominates Greece.

336 Philip murdered. Alexander becomes king of Macedonia. The Classical period ends and the Hellenistic period begins.

334-323 Alexander founds his empire, invading and defeating the Persian empire.

323 Alexander dies at Babylon and his huge empire is split by his generals. Ptolemy takes Egypt and Seleucus takes Persia.

200 The age of Greek scientific discovery follows, based around Alexandria in Egypt.

100 Rome gains power in Asia as the Greek civilization declines.

30 Cleopatra, the last ruler of Ptolemy's family, loses her Egyptian kingdom to Rome.

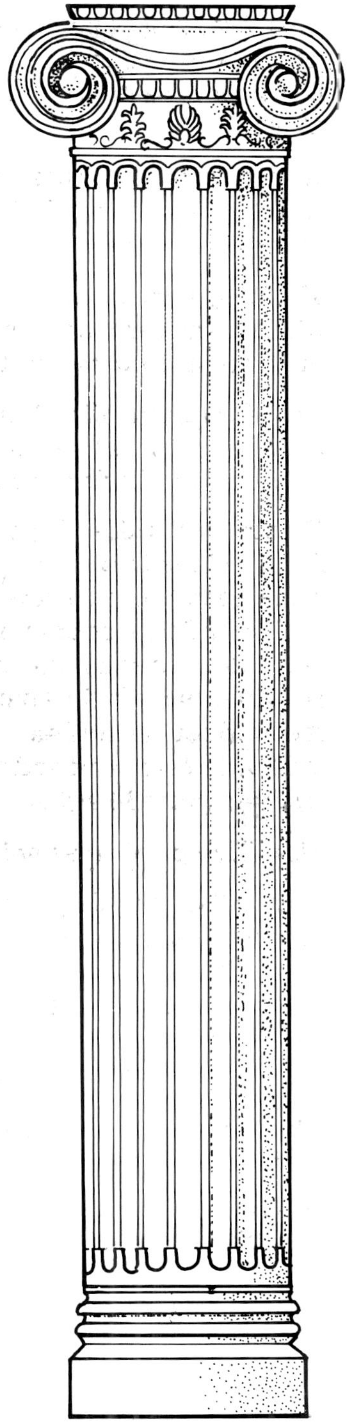

Glossary

abacus: a frame with rows of sliding beads on wires or in groves, which is used for counting
administration: the management or organization of something
amphidromia: a ceremony at which a baby is named. Today, we call this the 'christening'
apprentice: someone who works for a skilled person in return for being taught that skill
archaeologist: a person who finds out about the past by studying old buildings and objects
aristocracy: a country, or part of a country which is ruled by a small group of its richest and most powerful people
auloi: a V-shaped Greek musical instrument made of two pipes which were both blown into at once. One was then played with the right hand and one with the left

cavalry: soldiers on horseback who fought outside the group of foot soldiers
ceremony: a formal ritual or occasion. The parts of a ceremony usually follow a strict pattern or order
chiton: a simple tunic or robe made from two lengths of cloth fastened together at the shoulders and belted at the waist
citizen: any member of a country, or part of a country, who is allowed to take part in choosing its rulers
city-state: part of a country which includes the city at its centre and the countryside around it. Each city-state had its own ruler
civilization: to live according to a series of rules and laws. Civilizations are made up of groups of people who live together and obey the same rules
colony: a group of people who settle away from their own country, but still consider themselves to be part of it
cosmetics: substances used on the skin, especially the face, which are intended to improve a person's appearance. Today, we usually call this make-up
culture: the ways in which a civilization improves itself and develops. Different countries grow up in different ways, so they all have different cultures

democracy: a country or part of a country which is ruled by a group of people chosen by all its citizens

fortify: to make stronger. A fortified town is one protected by a strong wall which is built around it
foundations: the base on which a building stands. Foundations, usually built under the ground, are needed to support a building properly

herbalism: the study and use of herbs for treating illness
himation: a type of shawl, worn by the women of ancient Greece over a tunic. The himation was usually made of wool
Hippocratic Oath: the oath, or promise, created by Hippocrates, as a code of correct behaviour for people who treat the sick. Doctors still have to take this oath today before they can practise medicine

interest: extra money charged by a bank or money lender, on top of the amount loaned. The interest is a payment for the use of the bank's money
invest: to put money into something. Investors hope to make more money from their investment

league: a group of people or countries who share the same beliefs and have the same aims
linen: a type of cloth made from the woven fibres of the flax plant

mosaic: a design or picture made of small pieces of coloured stone, glass or clay
myth: a legend, or traditional story, which is based on fantasy rather than the truth

obol: a silver coin of ancient Greece
oligarchy: a country, or part of a country, which is governed by only a few of its people
oracle: a place where people could consult the gods, usually through a special priest or priestess who might also be known as the oracle

peltasts: lightly armed soldiers who fought on either side of the main body of soldiers in battle
phalanx: the formation in which the hoplites, or foot soldiers, fought in battle
philosopher: someone who seeks the truth, a thinker

Renaissance: a new beginning. A period during the fourteenth century when people emerged from the Dark Ages and began to study the art and thinking of Classical Greece

sanctuary: a holy place. Churches and temples are sanctuaries
sculpture: a work of art, which is carved or moulded, rather than painted. Statues are sculptures
shrine: a place, or object, which is considered important enough to be worshipped. A shrine is often inside a temple
surgery: cutting into part of a person's body to treat or remove something
symposium: a drinking party and talk held after a feast. Symposiums were often accompanied by musical entertainment

tenant farmer: a farmer who does not own the land he works. He may rent it or be employed by the owner
terrace: a flat area which is not level with the ground. Vines are often grown on a series of terraces, cut into a hillside like large, shallow steps
threshold: a point of entry to a building. The threshold is usually a plank or stone at the bottom of the door into a house
trireme: a Greek warship with sails and three rows of oars, one above the other

yarn: long spun thread which is prepared for weaving, knitting or sewing

Index